THE HELPERS

SOMETIMES IT'S DANGEROUS TO ASK FOR HELP...

WILLIAM HORICK

outskirtspress
DENVER, COLORADO

This is a work of fiction. The events and characters described herein are imaginary and are not intended to refer to specific places or living persons. The opinions expressed in this manuscript are solely the opinions of the author and do not represent the opinions or thoughts of the publisher. The author has represented and warranted full ownership and/or legal right to publish all the materials in this book.

The Helpers
Sometimes It's Dangerous to Ask for Help...
All Rights Reserved.
Copyright © 2014 William Horick
v4.0

Cover Photo © 2014 thinkstockphotos.com. All rights reserved - used with permission.

This book may not be reproduced, transmitted, or stored in whole or in part by any means, including graphic, electronic, or mechanical without the express written consent of the publisher except in the case of brief quotations embodied in critical articles and reviews.

Outskirts Press, Inc.
http://www.outskirtspress.com

ISBN: 978-1-4787-3204-4

Outskirts Press and the "OP" logo are trademarks belonging to Outskirts Press, Inc.

PRINTED IN THE UNITED STATES OF AMERICA

We are the music makers,
And we are the dreamer of dreams,
Wandering by lone sea-breakers,
And sitting by desolate streams,
World-losers and world-forsakers,
On whom the pale moon gleams,
Yet we are the movers and shakers
Of the world forever, it seems.

The Ode From Music and Moonlight
By Arthur O'Shaughnessy (1844-1881)

Chapter One
Encounters

B RIGDON MUNSEFORD CHONLIFF and I are not your standard *good old boys*. In our twilight years we like to think of ourselves as men of sterling character who have made notable contributions to the frenetic human race.

Our wives keep hanging such accolades upon us, and we never bother to dispute their proud claim. They are twin sisters who look exactly like the Hollywood legend, Hedy Lamarr. So Brigdon and I have much better things to do with them than contradict their opinion about us.

We did not always the twins. Before they snuggled into our saddle sore lives, Brigdon and I kept trying to ignore a pile of hackneyed labels that made the big stack of our years sound like the ultimate zilch. That however was impossible. Like Jack Lemmon and Walter Matthau of movie fame, we became known as *grumpy old men*. On our downhill slope of life the collection spread like liver spots. People were always ready to wag their testy tongues at us with old, mildewed hoots. We were called, in no particular order, old codgers, old geezers, old goats, and old coots.

Nor should I omit *old farts* from that canticle of derision.

But whatever the tag, Brigdon Chonliff and Homan Lloyd Kandall continued to find that World Series of taunts totally unacceptable.

You see, we had already crowned ourselves with nothing so blandly trite. Being innovative and creative, we bemoaned our social decline and aging process with a phrase we activated with a good dose of humor. We patronized each other as a couple of old sticks poking through the dirt pile of life in search of that lost coin called pride.

In all truth, Brigdon and I finally endured even that verbal dart we flung at ourselves. Now it really makes no difference what nit-picking people call us. We have a radical zest for life, and that's all that ultimately matters.

The twins remind us of that every blessed day. Brigdon and I rightfully call them our *helpers*.

He and I discovered these darlings when we turned 70-something, and our hoarfrost years have been a fling ever since. Now a lot of young studs are pea green with envy over the quick-step, the frolic in life we enjoy, thanks to those daring young women who became our wives.

This chronicle then is our story, Brigdon's and mine, but it also dutifully and beautifully belongs to those ladies of valor and faith who stormed across the mote and into the castle of our retreat where life had become an obnoxious cobweb that neither Brigdon or I could brush away.

It all began when Brigdon Chonliff and I started sharing life, with all of its absurd pokes and pulls, upon our arrival on the Baylor University campus in early September of 1946. World War Deuce was over, and we were a couple of

THE HELPERS

its has-beens, two ex GIs who were entwined into that vast throng that one day would be called *The Greatest Generation* of Americans who fought to make the world again safe for that elusive doodad called *democracy*.

We became good friends when we moved into a little shanty of an apartment on Speight Avenue near the campus. It wasn't much of a beehive, but it was perfect for Brigdon and me. It was away from the turmoil of campus life where freshman beanies and green and gold t-shirts were so numerous. He and I were part of the large freshman class, a class that would help thrust Baylor out of its tight little island and martinet atmosphere, but we wanted no part of its buzz. As veterans, Brigdon and I could live off-campus and pursue our major in Journalism without paying homage to freshman rituals. So we tried to dislodge ourselves from that gimcrack scene as much as possible.

For Brigdon Chonliff, that became increasingly difficult. There were too many attractive co-eds floating around the campus for him to ignore. When we met while standing in a registration line at the remodeled Army barracks Baylor called its Journalism Department, he revealed his lifelong intent to me.

"I plan to devote myself to chasing women here at Baylor", he said. "I want to become a photographer after college who captures the allure of pretty faces and curvy figures. In doing that, I shall pursue the almighty dollar as every good capitalist does. But for now, I'll be quite content to investigate all the lovely chicks here on campus who may cluck for a nocturnal allegiance."

"And that's why you came to Baylor?" I asked him.

He grinned. "That and Baylor's colors. All this green and gold reminds me of money. It's a beautiful sight."

In the war, Brigdon had been a waist gunner on a B-17 that flew daylight bombing missions over Germany. He was a sandy-haired little pepper pot from Amarillo who had a loquacious mouth. To hear him account for his combat experiences, you would almost believe this guy personally shot down every German aircraft that attacked his B-17.

Brigdon also claimed that he had divested a lot of English maidens of their virginity while his bomber squadron was based in the countryside of their homeland.

But now, Brigdon Chonliff had a whole new world to conquer sexually.

"I see this campus as a fertile field of sugar plum sweeties just waiting for the Chonliff swoop," he explained one morning as we viewed the skirt parade in the Student Union Building."

"That figures," I replied. "After all, you were a tail gunner in the war."

"A waist gunner," he corrected. "On a B-17 there was a big difference between the tail and the waist."

"But there's not much of a difference in a woman's anatomy is there? Waist or rear, you're still gunning for the same target, aren't you?"

"Know something, Kandy? That's what I like about you. Your humor is so devastatingly subtle."

Unlike Brigdon Chonliff, I was extremely tranquil about my role in the war. I had been a Navy *old salt*, a Signalman Third who was with Admiral Ray Spruance's aircraft carrier flotilla in the titanic and telltale battle of Midway Island. In that mighty clash we kicked Admiral Yamamoto's butt. That became a stunning defeat for the Japanese fleet. But my ship, the *Yorktown*, did not survive. For months after the battle, I still relived the carnage in my mind, the bombs, the exploding fuel, the maimed bodies and seared flesh. I was one of the crew members lucky enough to dive into the uneasy safety of the foul sea when the order came to abandon ship.

Nor did Homan Kandall have any delusions of sexual grandeur on the Baylor campus that possessed my apartment roommate so pointedly. I needed no such frills, even though I was a tall good-looking dude who had a wavy wad of dark hair and mirthful green eyes. I already had a steady girlfriend. My childhood sweetheart, Maydell Collins, was a junior Voice major at Baylor who also played in the band. Maydell was, in fact, the primary reason I chose to follow the GI Bill to the school.

Even so, Baylor was the kind of small, private university that I preferred, and Waco was hardly more than an old two railroad, King Cotton town on the Brazos River that exuded its piety and revered its fame as a hotbed for high school football.

There was also another factor in my choosing Baylor.

The city's daily newspaper had one of the best-known sportswriters in Texas, an irascible grouch named Hex Grantham who loved tormenting readers and fellow scribes alike. With my burning flair to become the new Grantland Rice, I felt like I could learn more about sports writing from Hex Grantham than I ever could in any journalism class. All I had to do was find a way to puncture his gruff, hard-shelled exterior. And that, I had been told, was harder than counting the quills on a porcupine.

Early in that fall semester, I met Maydell late one afternoon at Waco Hall, a copious building that symbolically linked Baylor University to the city. She and I sat on one of its high steps holding hands as we talked, quite oblivious to everyone but ourselves. My lean, hard body surged with desire as it always did when Maydell sat close to me. My eyes revealed that I wanted something more than her hand. But we both had agreed to wait until the bed of our wedding night. Still, the way she loved to tousle my hair with her long fingers, as she did at that moment, often made me wonder if we could honor our pact.

With or without the massage of her fingers, Maydell was an excellent conversationalist. That I always admired because it enabled us to communicate freely and openly about our future. She was a pert and bouncy blonde forever bubbling with life. That, I think, was why she cherished music the way she did. For Maydell Collins, music was life-giving, a healing supportive force, and she had a spirited, melodious voice to send it soaring.

I did think she wasted her musical talent by playing flutes and piccolos in Baylor's Golden Wave Band. They seemed like insignificant little instruments to me. But Maydell played them with such gusto that I knew I would attend the upcoming concert for which Maydell and her fellow bandsmen had just finished a lengthy rehearsal on the Waco Hall stage.

"How was the rehearsal?" I asked.

"It was fine. As an encore at the concert, we're going to play *Stars And Stripes Forever*. You'll really enjoy that, won't you?"

"Sure. But sweetheart, you are a healthy, well-built all-American girl. You were my real life girl next door when we were growing up. You ought to play a big sound instrument, a trombone maybe. Then you'd be heard, whatever the band plays."

Maydell scolded me with her serious brown eyes.

"Don't you realize John Philip Sousa wove a solo for piccolos into his greatest march? The rest of the band is just background music while we tweet-tweet-tweet our special part."

"And you're proud of that?"

"Of course I am," she sighed. "I think people are a lot like piccolos. We are called to perform in life's concert with what we have to offer, even in a limited way. We have a cue that we dare not miss. Our solo performance adds depth to someone else's life, just like the way the piccolo section comes front and center near the rousing climax of *Stars And Stripes Forever*. It's that ingredient in life that I call caring and sharing."

"Maydell, I truly admire your nobility. But I certainly have no inclination to share you with anyone else."

"Not even with your roommate in that eyesore apartment where you're living?" she laughed.

"Especially not with Brigdon Chonliff," I said soberly.

"I've heard all about him. I think every girl on the campus already knows about his reputation, and this is just the first month of school. My fellow piccolo player in the band hasn't encountered your buddy, but she calls him the Great Wolf."

I squeezed Maydell's hand. "All the more reason I think

I should slip an engagement ring on your pinkie. I want Brig to know you're off limits."

"Homan, when you do, I shall wear it proudly because I'll know I'm engaged to a special guy who one day is going to be a great writer. Maybe not a sportswriter, but you will write things that capture the very fullness of people, that thing that's called soul. I know you will because I see that dedication in your eyes, the same dedication that I know lives inside you. That's the God-given purpose you have for living, just as it was God's purpose for you to survive the Yorktown."

I humbly accepted Maydell's perspective. In return I gave her a sneaky little kiss. The kiss would have had more lust to it, had it not happened in broad daylight on the steps of Waco Hall, so sacrosanct in the mindset of Baylor University.

While I said goodbye to Maydell, the Great Wolf was saying hello to a demure little brunette named Fredrica Foster in the campus bookstore. She happened to be the piccolo player Maydell had mentioned, a sophomore from Corpus Christi.

Fredrica Foster knew she had been followed across the campus even though Brigdon kept his distance behind her as they walked. She hastened her pace and then ducked into the bookstore. Brigdon leisurely entered with no apparent wolfish motive. He casually examined a book display, but when Fredrica halted between two racks of books, Brigdon made his pounce, confident the power of his old voodoo would prevail.

Their eyes locked when he and Fredrica faced each other in the narrow confine of the book racks. In his predatory stance, Brigdon liked Fredrica's gentle frown. It was not the militant frown he had anticipated. Instead, it gave her delicate, attractive face a lilt he could appreciate. It seemed to indicate she was prepared to accept his approach with only a slight annoyance. That caused him to veer away from his usual strategy. He saw in Fredrica Foster something more than a fly by night relationship. He would later admit that Fredrica Foster had her own kind of voodoo.

"I expected a hostile frown," he said. "I'm Brigdon Chonliff."

"I guessed that when you followed me in here. I've heard of you and your reputation, Mr. Chonliff."

He stepped closer to her. That caused the bookstore manager to ease into the aisle. He wanted no hanky-panky in his store.

"I think you had better move along, young man," he said. It's obvious you're bothering this student."

"Was I bothering you?" Brigdon asked.

"Knowing your reputation, Mr. Chonliff, I think that's exactly what you intended."

Brigdon waited for Fredrica Foster outside the bookstore. He walked beside her as she strolled toward her dorm.

"I was sure you would be waiting for me," she said.

"I had to. I didn't want my infamy to sour you. I'm really a nice guy, a lonely ex GI seeking some feminine companionship while I patrol these hallowed precincts of old Baylor."

Fredrica was not impressed. "That's a very good line, Mr. Chonliff, but I know your type. I'm majoring in Sociology."

"All right, that's good. Now you can be my case worker. I'll tell you all about my background up in cold Amarillo on famous Route 66 where I played cowboy on my father's ranch before the war. You'll get to know the real me. Okay, does that rate a date with you? Honestly, I'm not interested in any sexual escapade. Not now. Not anymore. I want you to understand that."

Her reply startled him. "Very well, you can take me to church Sunday morning."

"Uh, church-going is against my religion."

"What is your religion, Mr. Chonliff?"

Brigdon looked nonplussed. "I don't really know. I've never been in church anywhere enough to know, not even during the war when I had perilous flights in a B-17."

"I appreciate your frankness," said Fredrica. "But don't you think it's time you found religion? I cannot believe the Lord wants you to still wallow in the hog pen that has been your predatory way of life."

Thus began the transformation of Brigdon Munseford Chonliff.

He joined Fredrica's church that Sunday morning, and then the campus coeds either breathed a sigh of maximum relief, or else churned an inquisitive mind about how the little piccolo player in the Golden Wave Band had managed to pluck the Great Wolf away from their erotic fantasies.

Maydell and I began double-dating with Brigdon and Fredrica. On those nights when we didn't cozy up to our gals in the balcony of the Waco Theatre, Brigdon and I treated them to an evening at *Harry B's*, the off-campus watering hole for a lot of Baylor students, including half the football team. Or so it was thought.

One night while Brigdon and I swigged our *cool ones*, I

THE HELPERS

offered a lengthy recital about old movies and the character actors who were so well-known in their supporting roles. The girls listened intently as they sipped their *Canada Dry* ginger ales, but Brigdon concentrated on draining his beer.

"Those actors and actresses are countless," I said. "They're just like stars in a nocturnal sky. And whatever their movie role might be, you remember them and love them."

"Names. Give us names," said Brigdon, his voice a bit agitated because his beer had become tepid. "Who were these immortals?"

Maydell swallowed another drab of her ginger ale.

"That's your cue, sweetheart," she smiled. "Put up or shut up."

I accepted her challenge. "Okay, for a starter, how about Donald Meek, the little baldy so aptly named. He was the milquetoast whiskey salesman in *Stagecoach*, the movie that brought John Wayne into full stardom."

"I remember that movie," said Maydell. "But who played the bad guy that John Wayne killed in the gunfight?"

"That was Tom Tyler. He played in a lot of old B-grade cowboy westerns before *Stagecoach*."

Brigdon scowled. "Who else? What about Elmer Fudd, who's always bamboozled by Bugs Bunny?"

With the girls nodding their approval, I rattled off the names in staccato-like fashion. "Henry Travers, Jack Elam, John Carradine, and Anthony Quinn. Now there's a man who can play any role and any nationality. Before he's through, Anthony Quinn will have leading roles in a lot of major films. He'll be a Hollywood immortal."

"Do tell," said Brigdon. He waved his glass at our waiter to indicate his thirst for a refill. But when he saw Fredrica give him the same gentle frown he had seen in the bookstore, Brigdon waived the waiter away.

I marveled at how Fredrica Foster had already become a steadying influence on him.

Fredrica relaxed and smiled. "Homan, you haven't mentioned Max Steiner. Maydell bet me that you surely know about Max Steiner."

I glanced at Maydell who verified the wager. I chalked up an imaginary plus sign for her.

"Max Steiner happened to be an exceptional composer," I said. "He wrote the music for *Gone With The Wind*, *Casablanca*, and *Dark Victory* for which Bette Davis won an Oscar as best actress. Max Steiner and his music are rightfully lodged among the greats of Hollywood."

To console himself, Brigdon emptied his glass. He wiped the residue off his lips with his tongue.

"Only you two piccolo tooters could come up with somebody named Max Steiner," he snorted. "You should have asked Hollywood Homan about Hedy Lamarr."

"Let's save Hedy for our next little binge here at *Harry B's*," I suggested. "Then I'll tell you about her role as Tondelayo."

Brigdon Chonliff and I did not then know that one day in our autumnal years two magnificent later editions of Hedy Lamarr would merge into our lives.

Chapter Two
Mr. Grantham

EARLY IN our freshman year Brig and I decided to jumpstart our journalistic careers. We agreed to venture uninvited into the private lair of the gruff, antagonistic Hex Grantham. It would be risky like diving into a piranha pool, we realized. But we felt the encounter with the sour-faced old sportswriter would be better than any classroom lecture. And we were correct.

Orville Hexley Grantham was seated in a back booth the Thursday night Brigdon and I found him in his favorite bar. It was a dimly lit hole-in-the-wall joint across the street from *The Waco Clarion*. We had heard that Hex Grantham enjoyed this isolation from staffers on the paper and any other intruders who dared to foist themselves into his privacy. He scowled when he saw us come into Charlie's Bar.

Brig and I feared the worst as we eased toward his booth.

The venerable sports editor had a furrowed brow and small, beady eyes. He was short and dumpy like most of the lines he wrote in his daily columns. A cigarette dangled between his lips as he skimmed through an early edition of *The Clarion*. He, however, was not the ogre we expected. The old scribe became quite amiable when he sensed the reason we had invaded his den. He could even quote Shakespeare, Brig and I soon discovered. He could also dish out slivers of profanity at times.

He invited us to slide into his booth for his appraisal.

"You're from Baylor, aren't you? War veterans, I presume."

Brig and I nodded a bit apprehensively, unsure of Hex Grantham's mood for ex GIs. His age and heart murmurs had kept him out of the war. So he had remained a civilian, and we knew that some civilians despised guys in uniform.

Hex Grantham flashed a weak smile. "That's good because I don't like being log-jammed by moony-eyed jellybeans right out of high school with their sugar sweet idealism. They're a pain in the butt."

"We lost our idealism when we fought in the war, Mr. Grantham," I said. "I hope we can regain it as Journalism majors at Baylor. We would like to work for the Waco *Clarion* some day. That's why we risked coming into your personal hideaway to meet you."

"That's right, Mr. Grantham," Brigdon added.

Hex quickly doused his cigarette into an empty beer glass.

"Well, the first thing you need to learn is don't call me Mr. Grantham. Or Orville. I'm known as Hex. That's my trademark, my identity, and I damn near worship it. Shakespeare said, *To thine own self be true.* You have to be that when you enter the newspaper jungle. Otherwise, you're not worth a tinker's damn to yourself or your paper."

Hex leaned back and pulled a fresh cigarette from the pack in his shirt pocket.

THE HELPERS

"Okay, who are you would-be typewriter jockeys? I admire your gumption for tracking me down here at Charlie's. Most people know I don't like being shaken out of my comfort zone back here. But if you're here for an interview, Charlie's little grotto is better than the hullabaloo across the street in the city room. So what's your spiel?"

Brigdon hoped his information would be worth the offer of a beer. "My name is Brigdon Chonliff. I'm interested in photographic journalism."

"I'm Homan Kandall," I said. "I want to be a sportswriter."

"With a name like that, I could have guessed," said Hex. "It does have a certain lilt to it. And hey, it damn well rhymes with Roman candle. You may well light up the sky with that name, son. Chonliff, I think you also have a great name. It makes you sound like some English lord from Devonshire."

Brig and I smiled at each other. We were absolutely sure we had piled up a lot of Brownie points with Hex Grantham.

He folded his copy of the *Clarion* early edition as he puffed on his fresh cigarette. He then wrote our names on the top of the front page and folded the paper again. It appeared the paper was ready to be trashed and us with it. Hex pushed the *Clarion* away and spoke again, his voice now agitated.

"Guys like you do face a potential problem. There's bound to be another war, or perhaps a series of wars. I think it's inevitable. That damned Russian bear has a big, dangerous paw. There's also the menace of Red China."

Hex slapped the newspaper against the corner of his booth. "Those communist bastards will stir the cauldron just like those witches in *Macbeth*. But if you boys stay at

Baylor and don't go traipsing off to some new global conflict to save the dignity of that scabby UN, come see me before you graduate."

We assured Hex Grantham that we would. We also had a question for him.

"Hex, everyone's picking Baylor to win Saturday," I said. "Why are you predicting the Bears will lose?"

Hex took a long drag on his cigarette. "Son, that's just part of my style. I actually think Baylor can win, but I like to grind up the fans occasionally. I enjoy letting them think they're smarter than me. If they despise me enough and often enough, they'll keep reading my column just to find a reason to make their scurvy comments. Let them loathe me and call me a s.o.b. I don't care. I like being controversial. That helps sell papers."

Brigdon and I headed back to our apartment, still elated over our conversation with the elusive Hex Grantham.

"That man is a character," Brigdon said. "He could be a tyrant to work for. We would have to become fanatics like him. Besides that, he didn't even offer us a beer."

"He offered us something better than a beer," I replied. "Hex gave us a look at himself and the way people become. I think he's afraid of the future. He doesn't want to gloss it over with any pie in the sky. So that's why he writes the way he does. It's his shell, and it protects him. He's a lonely old guy, but he doesn't want to change. He's comfortable being who he is."

"Well, I'm glad we're not like Hex Grantham," Brigdon countered. "You and I want to have a love tryst with life. That will be our safety net from whatever the stinking future may bring."

"Whatever it brings, we'll have Freddie and Maydell to love. When you're in love, you don't grow old. Your age may eventually cause your body to look like a shriveled gherkin, but as long as you have someone to love, the future is no enemy."

"Kandy, have you ever thought about changing your major to Philosophy?"

I was still considering that question before I fell asleep that night. I knew I would still major in Journalism at Baylor. But I also knew it would not hurt to wax philosophical at times. That was the stuff implanted in every good writer.

And in my mind, Hex Grantham was better than good. He wasn't old school, nor was he the trumpeter for some new breed of sportswriters. Hex was his own man. *To thine own self be true,* he had told Brig and me.

I thanked old Bill Shakespeare for those immortal words before I blinked off to sleep.

Chapter Three
Engagements

MY ROOMMATE had a fabulous Thanksgiving that freshman year. For Brigdon, it marked another major change in his life. He supplied the details when he returned from Corpus Christi.

He had accepted Fredrica Foster's invitation to go home with her for the holiday weekend, an open date for Baylor football and the Golden Wave Band. Brig had been reluctant to make the trip because it meant meeting her father, Fredrick Foster, an Air Force bird colonel still in the active ranks. Freddie had shown Brig a picture of him in his dress uniform. In the picture, Brig saw an imposing figure of a career military man who commanded the utmost respect with an intolerant eye for any nonsense.

Any fears Brigdon had about the encounter were unfounded. He and Colonel Foster discovered they had an easy rapport with each other. They talked incessantly about the various airplanes that had a major role in the war.

Fredrick Foster thought the B-17E was the ultimate Flying Fortress, and that the German Messerschmit and the

THE HELPERS

Fouke-Wulf fighters were deadly foes. Brig lauded the B-25 bombers that led the Doolittle raid on Tokyo, and asked Colonel Foster what he thought about the merits of the P-51 Mustangs and the crazy looking P-38s who were hated by the Germans.

Their conversation resumed when they had coffee in the den after the Thanksgiving dinner. It finally culminated with a prolonged and frank discussion about the *Bomb*. Fredrick Foster was a staunch, active Republican, but he praised President Harry Truman for his decision to use the awesome weapon against Japan.

"Young man, you might not be here today if Truman had been gutless," he said.

"And I wouldn't like that," said Freddie as she entered the den. "Daddy, I'm glad Brigdon came back safe from the war. But I'm not sure he'll be safe from all those aerial photos you have that were taken during the war. May I have him for a little reconnaissance?"

"I would love to see those photos, sir" Brigdon said eagerly. He still wanted to stockpile more points with Fredrick Foster if possible.

"They can wait," the colonel smiled. "Right now I think my Air Force brat would like some time with you alone. I'll go help Mrs. Foster with the dishes, and maybe give her fanny a pinch in return for my service."

He picked up the coffee tray and gave Brig a jovial wink as he left.

With his exit from the den, Freddie slid closer to Brig on the cushioned couch that graced the paneled room.

"Don't let my father give you ideas about pinching my fanny, Brigdon Chonliff. Not until we're married, at least."

"I wouldn't think of it," said Brig. "And besides, you don't have much of a fanny to pinch. I noticed that when I followed you across the campus that afternoon. I didn't see any twisty-twisty in your walk."

"I didn't want to excite you."

"Excite me now."

Freddie feigned displeasure with his remark and tried to slap his head with a couch pillow. The half-hearted maneuver failed, but she hoped Brig would make a move of his own.

Brig did not disappoint her. His kiss was a long and salient feature of their mutual love that had flamed so quickly after they met in the Baylor bookstore.

"When do I resort to the old standard protocol of asking your father for your hand in matrimony," he said at last.

"Oh, can't you tell? That won't be necessary. You won't have to shoot down my father like he was one of those German fighter planes in the war. I have a hunch Daddy is telling Mom right now he highly approves of you."

"Not by pinching her fanny, I hope" Brig laughed.

He had more good news to report when I saw him again Sunday night.

Fredrick Foster had promised to help his start as a photographer after graduation at Baylor. Brig's interest in those aerial photos had opened that door.

"Okay, old fly boy, off you go into the marital wild blue yonder," I grinned. "Just don't parachute down on this old sea dog's deck when the flak gets heavy."

My own Thanksgiving had been much less eventful.

Maydell and I drove up to Waxahachie, our hometown,

early that morning. We had dinner at my parent's home with Maydell's folks and her 10 year old sibling brother, Geraud. He was a garrulous puddinhead who kept eyeing me during the family feast.

I kept thinking he wanted to ask me something. But Geraud remained aloof, and that for me was another Thanksgiving blessing. Maydell and I were not quite ready to announce our engagement, but everyone at the dinner table, including Geraud, surely knew the revelation would come soon in the very rapid prance of time.

That fullness of time came on Christmas Eve at the Collins' home. Their lavish living room was festively ripe with a towering fur tree that almost scraped the ceiling. With eggnog salutations, the two families exchanged gifts. It was a long process, but at last the stately tree had a barren underside. Maydell gave me a Smith Corona portable typewriter, and a light kiss was all that she received in return.

Everyone there, and especially Geraud, quickly sensed my neglect. Maydell opened her other gifts, but found nothing from me. Sitting close to the tree, she eyed me quizzically and probed the torn wrapping papers around her feet. As she continued her sudden frantic search, she realized there was no misplaced gift amid the clutter. I could see the almost tearful hurt in her brown eyes.

"Is this what you're looking for", I asked as I pulled a small, gift-wrapped box from the pocket of my jacket. "Here, catch", I said casually while tossing the box to her.

Maydell knew what the box contained even before she opened it. With her usual dexterity, she leaped into my arms. She gleefully allowed me to place the ring on her finger.

"With this ring I thee engage," I said merrily.

"With this ring, you now have a fiancée," Maydell laughed. "It's a lot better than that cigar wrapper you gave me in the fifth grade. I gladly accept this gift right here in front of our families, including my wide-eyed kid brother, God, and Santa Claus. Then tomorrow I'll spread my Christmas joy to everyone else in this quaint little city of Waxahachie."

She then flitted around the tree, showing off her prize to everyone. Only Geraud eyed it with any sense of disdain. I knew he and Maydell were close despite their age range difference. He probably would not be happy losing his big sister to me.

Maydell and I spent nearly an hour accepting the plaudits of our parents and talking about future wedding plans. Mrs. Collins even shared her fresh Christmas cheer with a phone call to her brother in Nashville. But she had to brush away some joyful tears during the conversation.

Geraud declined to join the family greetings during the call. I was the center of his attentive stare.

We finally feasted on hot homemade tamales and Mexican rice. The tamales were a Christmas Eve gift from some Hispanic friends named Fuentes who gave it each year as an honored Yuletide tradition. Everyone bowed in reverence to the Almighty before the dinner when Mr. Collins gave thanks.

Everyone, that is, except Geraud. I caught him peeking at me during the prayer. He was giving me the same questioning look that I had seen before.

After the tamale supper, Geraud finally invited me into his boyhood den, a room replete with pictures of his favorite sports idols. He carefully shut the door behind me.

"What is it, Geraud? I think you've got a bad case of the bothers."

His reply was open and candid. "Why are you gonna marry my sister?"

"That's an easy question. Because I love her, that's why."

"Oh, really? Then I bet you've already seen her nakid."

"You're certainly an inquisitive pup, Geraud. But no, I have never seen your sister naked. And I won't until we're married."

Geraud pressed on. "But I bet you saw a lot of nakid women when you wuz in the Navy."

I tried to parry his comment with humor.

"Why, of course. All I had to do was wave my semaphore flags and they came running to me without a stitch."

That did not faze this kid. Nothing ever seemed to whittle him down to size.

"Well, I'm better than you," he said. "Last year when I was just nine years old, I saw Maydell nakid. She didn't know it, but I peeked at her one time through the bathroom door when she stepped out of the shower."

"She didn't spot you?"

Geraud took a deep breath as if to atone for his sin.

"Heck no. She woulda skint me alive if she had."

I found myself warming up to this puddinhead who looked like *Alfalfa* in those old *Our Gang* comedies in the movies.

"So what did you think when you saw her naked?"

He eyed me with a mischievous smile. "I thought then, an' I still do, golly gee. I've sure gotta good lookin' sister. You won't ever tell her about this, will ya"?

"Scout's honor," I pledged. "But Geraud, good buddy, you are so right. You do have a beautiful sister, but Maydell is lovely just the way you and I see her every day. She's not a girl who will ever have to shed her clothes to show her good looks. Her real beauty is inside her. That's why I love her. You will understand that some day."

Geraud opened the door and took my hand.

"Come on, Homan. Let's go peel some more of those hot tamales. It's almost Christmas, good buddy."

Chapter Four
Something Hot and Spicy

P RESIDENT HARRY TRUMAN came to Waco early the next year to receive an honorary doctorate degree from Baylor University. It was a banner event for the city, of course. All the local radio stations kept playing *The Missouri Waltz* in Truman's honor prior to his arrival.

The ceremonial day began as a brutal March morning, chilled by a raw, north wind and intermittent rain. Maydell and Freddie stood beside Brigdon and me on South Fifth Street during our long wait for the presidential motorcade to come by. Freddie kept adjusting the green scarf around her neck as she tried to ward off the stabs of the churlish wind.

Brig gently draped his arm around her, but still she shivered.

"This weather is worse than Amarillo's," he snarled. "But at least it snows up there, which is better than this slop, and my old hometown does have some good Mexican restaurants. That's what we need today---a good Mexican restaurant down here close to the campus. Freddie, maybe some day you'll learn to cook Mexican food, and we'll have a thriving business that will bless old Baylor much more than this Truman hiatus."

He gave Freddie a tender kiss, not realizing it would be the final display of affection he would bestow upon her while she lived.

Freddie was too cold to appreciate Brig's kiss, nor did she savor his suggestion with any enthusiasm. "Yeah sure," she muttered forlornly.

The motorcade finally came into view, slowly poking along Fifth Street toward Waco Hall. We got a brief glimpse of the President as his vehicle, surrounded by Secret Service agents, moved past us. Brig and I stood at attention and saluted the man who had been our Commander-in-Chief during the war after the death of President Franklin Delano Roosevelt. Two members of the security detail gave us a hard look, but kept pace with the Truman limo.

As the parade moved past us, we decided some hot and spicy Mexican food would replace our shivers on that snotty March day. It would be our tribute to Harry Truman after our long wait for him on the cold, damp street. His visit provided a holiday from our Baylor classes, so we decided to have a leisurely meal at a cozy little café downtown on Seventh Street.

While we dined on enchiladas, rice, and chili, I mentioned Hedy Lamarr because she was also hot and spicy.

"In that movie *White Cargo*, she makes her entrance with this seductive line---'I am Tondelayo.' Friends, you may never hear such a sultry voice anywhere again."

Maybell hunched her shoulder toward me. "And I am provocative Maydell", she said in a low enticing voice. "Now

THE HELPERS

Homan Kandall, I suggest you forget about your precious Hedy."

Brig and I laughed. Freddie tried to laugh, but only coughed. It was a deep sounding cough that ripped her throat.

I glanced nervously at Freddie before I spoke again.

"Hedy was controversial. Before she came to Hollywood, she made a European movie called *Ecstacy*. In it Hedy did a nude scene, and I mean nude. She showed all of herself."

"Yeah, I saw that movie when I was in the Air Force," said Brig. "I thought, my God, why don't they make movies like that in Hollywood."

"They don't because our sense of decency would never accept such vulgar stuff," said Freddie. She coughed again. "I'm a Sociology major. I know what my professor would say about such degradation."

I nodded. "That's true for now, but I believe the aftermath of the war and any future war will undermine a lot of our prized cultural standards."

"You do?" Maydell asked as she bit into a cracker.

"I certainly do. I think a lot of movies in time will be more controversial than even Harry Truman. You likely will be seeing things and hearing words you would never imagine. Clark Gable started it in *Gone With The Wind* when he told Scarlett, 'Frankly my dear, I don't give a damn.' But that will be just a mild, four-letter snippet compared to others some screenwriters may include in their dialogue and far out story lines."

"Well Homan, now I'm glad you don't aspire to be a screenwriter," said Maydell. "It's okay to love those old movies like you do, but please don't ever write any sordid stuff for the movie screen."

"Oh, it won't be confined to screenwriters," I replied. "Old mores will drop their pristine pants and skirts everywhere in every social structure, even here in staid old Waco."

"Baylor will never approve of such changes," said Freddie. She tried to stifle another cough. "Our churches won't either."

Our waiter came by and refilled the cracker bowl on our table. He probably sensed our conversation evolved around a serious subject and that we were in no hurry to leave. He piddled around, still hoping that when we finally left, there would be a generous tip for him on the table.

"Freddie, I hope you're correct," I said. "But there may not be enough Billy Grahams to speak out against cultural erosions. Many churches, I think, will simply turn the other cheek, so to speak, and counter with a muffled rendition of *Onward, Christian Soldiers* and then quickly bless their congregation with some lollipop benediction. After it, the people will scurry off to the nearest Luby's cafeteria ahead of other church people who are also out for a good Sunday dinner. That and pro football will be the usual Sabbath showcase, I'm afraid.".

Brig grasped Freddie's hand and laughed.

"Sweetheart, if what Kandy says is true, why don't we kick tradition in the rump and elope to some nudist camp and get married there? Kandy, you and Maydell could make it a foursome."

"Brigdon, that's a very bad joke," said Freddie. "I would never settle for anything less than a traditional church wedding."

THE HELPERS

"Nor would I," Maydell declared rather sternly. "And besides, Baylor would never approve."

"That's right," I agreed. "But there's no way the university could stop us. We're individuals and we make individual choices. That's always been the scar on human conduct. That's why the Ten Commandments are largely ignored. Morality has never had a blue ribbon pinned on it. Morality has never had that pedigree rating. That was forever lost when Adam and Eve got booted out of their garden Shan-gri-la."

Freddie pushed her enchilada plate aside and looked wearily at us, shivering as she did.

"This whole conversation would make me sick, but I think I'm sick already. I'm chilled, but I feel hot and feverish." She shivered again as she spoke. "I really feel awful. My throat's so sore I can hardly speak."

Oh God, no, I thought to myself as I suddenly remembered the famous movie scene where Knute Rockne diagnosed the illness of his football star, George Gipp at Notre Dame. But this wasn't the movie version of the Gipper's terminal illness. It was instead, a scary premonition that dear little Freddie Foster could be very sick, and that we might easily lose her.

Maydell had heard me talk about the Knute Rockne scene. She instinctively felt Freddie's forehead.

"Sweetie, you do have a fever. I'm taking you to the campus infirmary right now. Homan, you and Brigdon can catch a bus back to Baylor."

He and I sat sullenly at our table after they left. We tried to finish the remnant of our meal, but with a mutual foreboding, we signaled the waiter for our check.

"She'll be all right", I said weakly as we walked outside.

The way Brig looked at me revealed his prognosis was entirely different.

"Damn this rotten day," he said at last.

In 1947 penicillin and other antibiotics were just then coming into prominence as wonder drugs. They were hailed as miracle workers. But unfortunately, some diseases were resistant to their power, especially in people whose immune systems were too low for those drugs to be life-saving.

Fredrica Foster, petite and pretty, was one of those unfortunate individuals. She lost her battle with viral pneumonia. The Baylor people had rushed her to the Hillcrest Hospital after her brief stay in the infirmary, but the medical team could not save her life. She died there two days before her 20th birthday.

Brigdon stood with the Fosters at her bedside and watched her breathe her last breath. It was a peaceful death with a wan smile creasing Freddie's lips while Brig held her hand. I watched at the foot of her bed as he placed an engagement ring on her finger moments after her death.

"Son, keep the ring," said Fredrick Foster. "You will eventually find someone else to wear it."

"No, Colonel. The ring was going to be her birthday present from me. I want her to be wearing it when she arrives at the Pearly Gates."

"That's very thoughtful of you," said Phyllis Foster with tears trickling down her patrician face. She came over to his side of the bed and kissed him fully.

"Brigdon, Colonel Foster and I know you were perfect

for Freddie, and would have been a wonderful son-in-law for us."

Brigdon Chonliff, the erstwhile Air Force hotshot who liked to pop off about his sexual exploits, flopped into a chair and sobbed bitterly.

I stood beside him sharing his grief, a grief of heavy remorse for both of us. I knew Brig had lost the love of his life, short though it was. There in the sadness of that hospital room, I was thankful that Maydell was strong and healthy.

Baylor University lovingly spent time and resources in expressing its sorrow for Freddie's death. The administration sent its condolences to the Fosters, and helped them arrange the funeral at the large Baptist church across the street from the campus, the church where Brig and Freddie shared their first date. Two school vice-presidents attended the service. Members of the Golden Wave Band gathered *en mass*, clad in their bright green and gold uniforms. A lot of Freddie's classmates also filed into the church for the funeral.

Brigdon sat with the Fosters and other family members in the front pews of the church. They heard Maydell salute Freddie with a piccolo rendition of *Amazing Grace*.

After the pastor's message about accomplishments in a short-lived life, a Music School soprano sang the inspiring *You'll Never Walk Alone*, a song Freddie had always admired. I thought the lyrics were so very appropriate:

> **When you walk through a storm, hold your head up high, and don't be afraid of the dark. At the end of a storm there's a golden sky and the sweet silver song of a lark.**

Walk on through the wind, walk on through the rain, though your dreams be tossed and blown. Walk on, walk on, with hope in your heart, and You'll never walk alone. You'll never walk alone.

I was seated directly behind Brig. When he began to quiver as the song reached its crescendo, I placed my hands on his shoulders.

"Just remember what Maydell likes to say," I whispered. "Caring is sharing. She and I share your loss with you."

At the Oakwood Cemetery following the committal and benediction, Fredrick Foster pulled Brig aside. The colonel carried Freddie's piccolo in its small case. I was able to hear their conversation.

"Son, I want you to have her piccolo," Colonel Foster said. "You wouldn't take back the ring, but please keep this instrument as a reminder of Freddie. Perhaps some day you will find someone who is worthy to play it, and then you'll be glad to give it to that person."

"Yes sir, I'll be happy to do that." It was an aimless reply.

"And please, Brig. Don't blame yourself about Freddie's death. She was always fragile. Phyllis and I nearly lost her when she was seven. But she survived. And that created a fierce desire in her to come to Baylor and meet a special someone who would share her life and her passion to help other people. Son, that was her dream. Freddie accomplished half of that dream, and I think she gave you the other half. For her sake, please don't fumble it away."

Brig hugged Fredrick Foster's neck in a shining moment of camaraderie.

THE HELPERS

"Colonel, when Freddie died, I felt like I was shot down over Germany. I bailed out of my 17, but I felt like my parachute wasn't going to open. Right now, I don't think it did. But I do thank you, sir."

He stepped back and saluted Colonel Foster who returned the gesture crisply with military precision. It was an imposing scene because Freddie's father was wearing his old Air Force uniform.

I smiled at their formal manner of acceptance. There was a bond between them that I sensed would long endure. I also believed Freddie would approve. I pictured her smiling down from heaven upon them.

But that evening I began to worry about Brig. I left him at the cemetery, and had not seen him since. No one at our apartment complex had seen him, either. Maydell drove me to *Harry B's*, but the search there was also fruitless.

We finally found him at Charlie's.

Brig sat in the same booth where Hex Grantham was churning out copy on his portable typewriter. They seemed to be completely unmindful of each other's presence. Hex kept pecking away without looking beyond his small keyboard, while a cigarette dangled between his lips.

My roommate looked catatonic. He had ignored a bottle of beer in front of him. He clutched Freddie's piccolo case as if it were a newborn offspring.

Hex Grantham finally glanced at Maydell and me with a sigh of relief.

"Your friend's been sitting there like than for over an hour," he said. "What the hell's the matter with him? Is he a Baylor flunkout or something?"

— 33 —

"The girl who would have become his fiancée died. She was buried in Oakwood this afternoon," I said.

The old sportswriter doused his cigarette. "Oh, I'm truly sorry, Chonliff."

"We hope Brigdon hasn't been a nuisance, Mr. Grantham," said Maydell. "Homan and I have been looking for him. We finally decided he might be here."

Hex Grantham gave her a sardonic smile in recognition of her ignorance.

"Young woman, I'm surprised your boyfriend hasn't told you. I'm called Hex. Nothing else, just Hex. . .unless you choose to baste me with some salty cusswords like a lot of people do."

"Sorry, sir" Maydell gulped, her face turning blush red.

I hoped the exchange would bring Brig out of his funk, but he remained poker-faced and deathly silent. His only movement was repeated tender rubs of the piccolo case.

"Didn't he say anything when he came in and parked in your booth?" I asked.

Hex rolled the paper out of his typewriter.

"Yeah, he did. He asked me what I was writing. I told him an in depth article about the start of the new baseball season. That's when he froze up."

Brig suddenly thawed. He pushed the beer bottle aside and carefully placed the piccolo case beside him in the booth.

"When Hex mentioned baseball, it knifed me in the gut. Baseball has its squeeze play, and I immediately felt like a runner trapped between third base and home plate on a botched up squeeze play. The Heavenly Coach called it, and I got caught in the rundown. Hell, that's just how I feel about Freddie's death. The Heavenly Coach called the wrong play when he let her die."

"Did he, Chonliff?" Hex asked the question with his eyes riveted on Brig. "Perhaps you missed God's signal. Maybe you left third base too soon. You were safe there, but you perhaps caused the rundown. It could be that God had a purpose for your girl's death, and that's the signal you missed. Think about that for awhile, and learn to be a better base runner in life."

Hex turned his face toward me.

"Kandall, I suggest you write a feature story about the girl's death. It probably has a human interest slant that no obit writer across the street could ever imagine. But I believe you can because of your friendship with Chonliff. So write it with passion. Make it jerk a lot of heart strings. I'll talk to the city editor about it. He owes me a favor after pulling that damned straight flush on me the other night. Write that story, Kandall. Write it, and write it over until it makes you cry. You'll get a byline, I promise, but also something better than a byline."

Hex looked over his copy and placed another cigarette between his lips. He lit a match, but Maydell sprang to his side and aggressively blew it out. She yanked the cigarette out of his mouth before crushing it in a metal tray already filled with other discards. Hex tried to recover from his bewilderment, but Maydell pounced on him with a flurry of words.

"Hex Grantham, I've always heard what a frostbitten malcontent you were. I've been told how you like to hide behind that typewriter and chop people down to size with your brusque sports prose. But anyone who believes that is crazy. A few moments ago when you challenged Homan to write that story, I saw you for what you really are---an old softy with a heart that rebels against the gruff fence you've created around yourself."

Maydell replaced her words with a bold slide into Hex Grantham's lap. She brazenly looped her arms around his neck.

"Now Hex," she declared, "I'm going to brave that beer breath of yours and those smoke-stained lips and give you something you've been needing a long, long time."

Hex blinked heavily under the spell of her sultry kiss. It took him a full moment to shake loose from its effect. He gently pushed Maydell off his lap.

"Young woman, Baylor girls aren't supposed to do anything that scandalous. That dumb stunt could get you expelled."

Maydell straightened her blouse. "But it won't though, will it, Hex? You wouldn't want to see cute little, adorable me get into trouble, would you?"

She patted his cheek as she spoke.

He shrugged. "Not this time, at least. For Crissake, who are you?"

"I am Tondelayo, and I'm hot and spicy."

It was obvious that Hex Grantham was not familiar with Hedy Lamarr or her role in *White Cargo*. But he was impressed with Maydell's exotic voice.

"Well Tondelayo, for that brazen audacity you just displayed, you may call me Mr. Grantham. Just don't take any liberties with that privilege."

THE HELPERS

"I understand, Mr. Grantham."

The old softy reverted back to his old self. "All right then. Now get your butt outta here. And take these two peckerwoods with you. I've got to get back over to the buzzard nest. Tondelayo, you say? Hell, that's a dumb ass name if I ever heard one."

Hex called to me as we were leaving. "Kandall, remember to write that feature story. Maybe Tondelayo will help you with it. She's got a lot of high-spirited gumption, the kind of savvy I admire."

Brig was laughing when we stepped out of Charlie's.

"Know something, Kandy? I wish I could have snapped a picture of old Hex when Maydell scorched him like she did. That picture would have been one for any sports hall of fame. Thanks Maydell for inserting some life back into me."

I smiled and shook his hand. "Brig, it's nice having you with us again."

Chapter Five
Foamy Gurgling Water

MAYDELL COLLINS and I somehow endured our long, tedious engagement. We abstained from sex, but not without difficulty. I always had to wonder if our fellow students thought we were still virginal, the way we were frequently hugging and kissing on campus, and giving each other playful pats on our bottoms. I was sure that we did not conduct ourselves in concert with the traditional Baylor standards. But Maydell always flashed her engagement ring to quell the curiosity of onlookers who thought we were too gauche.

She graduated in 1948 *magna cum laude*, and we married that summer in our church in Waxahachie. Brig was there, of course, as my best man. Even so, it was my new brother-in-law who gave me my best sendoff. Geraud Collins, all spruced up for the wedding, nudged up to me before the ceremony.

"Now you'll see what I saw that time when I peeked through the bathroom door, won't you, good buddy?"

I did indeed find full pleasure seeing the contours of her

THE HELPERS

nude body that wedding night in Denton, Texas where we stayed on our way to the Grand Canyon.

For three honeymooning days we marveled at that magnificent creation in Arizona no human could have designed. On our return to Texas, after a stopover in Amarillo where we said hello to Brig, we discovered our west Texas motel happened to be located near a nudist resort.

The manager asked us if we would be interested in visiting the place.

"We would have to take our clothes off," Maydell asked incredulously.

He smiled. "You would look rather freaky if you didn't."

Our eyes asked us, *Why not?* We spoke, recalling what Brig had said in the Mexican restaurant about getting married in a nudist camp. Maydell said she thought Brig would be pleased that we chose to end our honeymoon as non-conformists.

The decision came quickly with decided perkiness.

Thus armed with globs of suntan lotion and the pioneer spirit of the West, Maydell and I spent the next day going *au naturel.* After the initial shock of seeing so many couples sans clothing and being their cohorts, we fully accepted the way we were. At the Grand Canyon we had been tourists in company with other tourists. But now we were free spirits in a cordon of other free spirits who cared nothing about anyone seeing the shape, size, or age of their bodies.

This was no sexual orgy. It was simply the feeling that, in shedding their clothes, the people were revealing themselves to their Creator as He had made them. They were not ashamed to show themselves in their grand and glorious buff. To the contrary, I think all of us there that day would have been negligent in our humanity if we had not allowed God to witness the joy of our freedom.

That afternoon while Maydell and I were hot-tubbing, an elderly couple joined us. Both the man and his wife were wizened shadows of how they may have looked in their young lives. However, they showed no embarrassment or concern. They quietly eased into the bubbling water beside us.

"You're newlyweds, aren't you?" the man asked.

"How can you tell?" I laughed.

"Oh, it's easy," his wife replied. "You see, newlyweds seldom come here. They prefer the privacy of their marital seclusion. We spotted you right after you arrived. You looked like, and acted like newlyweds."

"We sort of dared each other to do this," I said.

"You really shouldn't think of it as daring," the woman said. "This no clothes resort is a retreat from all the dares people have to face in the everyday world as they try to keep themselves out of the crazy house."

"She's right," the old gentleman affirmed. "I'm a retired minister, and also the chaplain here. In my ministerial career I saw lots of people knuckle under to life because they always accepted the crude, vulgar demands it made upon them. Too many of them never tried to find a safety valve. This resort is one of those safety valves."

Maydell suddenly stirred. "But sir, we can't run away from what God expects of us in life, can we?"

"No, we cannot. But that would be true only if God were hostile to this way of acknowledging Him, my dear," the chaplain corrected. "And God's grace won't allow that

THE HELPERS

hostility here. This foamy, gurgling water we're sitting in is a sample of that Divine grace. It is the Lord's way of replenishing us for all the tomorrows and their absurdities we must face fully clothed."

Our conversation continued for several minutes. The chaplain asked if either of us could entertain the camp that evening.

"We're having a talent show after a barbeque supper," he explained.

With an approving gesture from me, Maydell volunteered her musical ability. "I majored in Voice in college. Perhaps I can find something to sing at the party."

She and I climbed out of the hot tub. The old couple was oblivious to the swing and sway of our wet buttocks as we walked away.

If the couple had left before us, I knew Maydell and I would have also ignored their skinny shanks. It did not matter how their rear ends pitched and tossed, or ours. They were part of a human anatomy we had in common, and we would let God be the judge of them.

The chaplain introduced us to all the campers that evening. As the talent show emcee, he called Maydell to the dimly lit stage in the center of the resort. A middle aged woman sat at a piano, ready to accompany Maydell.

My dauntless bride captured the audience even before she sang. In show biz, that's called the ice-breaker, and Maydell mastered it adroitly.

"I'll tell you something about my husband," she said. "He has a very droll sense of humor. He thinks the great thing about being a nudist is that there are never any pickpockets around."

The campers burst into a solid wave of laughter.

"And I'll tell you something about his bride who isn't the blushing type anymore. I played a piccolo when I was in the Baylor University band. I still have it, and I still have my uniform. But as you can see quite clearly, I'm not wearing it or anything else here this evening."

When the laughter subsided, Maydell sang the lilting *I'll Be Seeing You*, long a sentimental favorite of many people.

> *I'll be seeing you in all the old familiar places*
> *this heart of mine embraces all the day through.*
> *In the small café, the park across the way,*
> *the children's carousel, the chestnut tree, the*
> *wishing well.*
> *I'll be seeing you in every lovely summer day,*
> *and everything that's bright and gay.*
> *I'll always think of you that way.*
> *I'll find you in the morning sun, and when the night*
> *is new, I'll be looking at the moon,*
> *but I'll be seeing you.*

Her audience applauded loudly when Maydell finished. She bowed to her fellow nudists and blew me a kiss. Then and there, that song became our song. Throughout our marriage, we would treasure it as a mutual tribute to the love we had for each other.

That night in our motel room, we heard numerous freight trains rumble past on the tracks across the highway. Those trains did not bother us an iota. We were on our own track as we rumbled blissfully together in bed.

True to the lyrics she had sung, Maydell found me in the morning sun the next day as it crept through the Venetian blinds of our window. I was still asleep, but the contented smile that came across my face when she touched me told us something. It revealed our joy in the fellowship of marital sex that had reached the zenith of erotic pleasure during the night.

Chapter Six
Recollections

THE ENSUING YEARS passed quickly, mostly without any campus fanfare. The GI Bill of Rights proved to be a financial godsend, although Maydell had become a choral teacher in one of Waco's elementary schools after her graduation. That helped us to live in a comfortable little upstairs apartment near downtown Waco.

Things were not going very well for Brigdon, although he did establish himself in photography and worked periodic free lance stints for *The Waco Clarion*. But he still lived in the same dinky apartment on Speight Avenue, and now by himself. He kept a picture he had taken of Freddie by his bed. It stood by her piccolo case. The Great Wolf was no longer feared as a campus hustler. With his thoughts continually on Freddie, Brig never dated again.

He told me about his reclusive stance.

"Freddie's picture and her piccolo case keep me churning along, Kandy. Know what I mean? I suppose they have become crutches, but they give me fond memories of her that I can't shake loose from my mind. What do you think?"

THE HELPERS

"Something will shake them loose. Some day, you'll find the shaker."

Brig and I still never got involved in campus activities, although we did enjoy our staff status on *The Daily Lariat*, the student newspaper that carried more ads than news within its runty four page format.

I once suggested to him that we should cover a nudist camp and bring some real news and photos to the *Lariat*.

"Kandy, like I've always said, your humor is always so beastly subtle," he smiled.

"Maydell calls it droll."

"Aw, who cares what flavor it is. I'm just thankful you can make me laugh. Promise that you always will. A nudist camp? Kandy, you would reel in horror seeing a lot of crazies without their clothes. How would you ever explain that to Maydell?"

I grinned limply. "Gosh, I never thought of that."

Some of our required courses gave Brig and me a few queasy times, especially Chemistry when we smoked everyone out of the lab one day with a test tube experiment that exploded on a hot Bunsen burner. But we passed those mind bogglers and picked up the necessary grade points en route to our senior year. During its months we concentrated solely on electives we needed to complete our major in Journalism. In the spring of 1950 our elation soared as we sped toward the finish line. We were not academic wizards flirting with the Dean's List. But neither were we a couple of lead-footed dingbats who had to stagger down the stretch laden with a heavy classroom load in quest of our BA degree.

A month or so before graduation, Hex Grantham called.

He invited me to come down to *The Clarion* for a consultation. I sat at his desk gaping around at the city room where a myriad of typewriters clicked out copy for the next edition.

Hex as usual had a cigarette sandwiched between his lips.

"Kandall, I asked you to come here instead of Charlie's for a special reason," he indicated. "You know why? I wanted you to get the feel of a city room. That's because if you follow the tip I give you, that's where you'll be earning your wampum."

"What kind of tip?"

"The daily paper out in Abilene is looking for a sports guy. I've talked to the sports editor about you, and he wants you to come in for an interview. Are you interested?"

"Well yes, of course," I stammered. "But Hex, I have always hoped to work for you, if you think I'm qualified."

"Kandall, I know quite well you're qualified. I've been reading some of the stuff you've tossed out for that campus rag at Baylor. Hell, I knew you could write back when you wrote that tear-jerker about that coed's death. Your friend Chonliff and I had a beer while we talked about how your story impacted *Clarion* readers."

"But you won't hire me?"

Hex Grantham leaned back in his chair and gazed at the ceiling of the city room.

"Son, I wish I could," he sighed heavily. "I've got a staff vacancy opening up, but the hitch is the paper's publisher. He has a young protégé. That kid probably doesn't know beeswax about writing good, potent copy, but the publisher is calling the play. So it's first and ten. We'll just have to wait for the fumble."

"I understand. Thanks Hex for your confidence in me."

"Well, don't waste time cryin' on my shoulder. Just grab a Greyhound and get your butt out to Abilene. Hey, it's a great sports town with three colleges and a high school football team that's steeped in tradition. Abilene High and Waco High had a great rivalry back in the 20s as you surely know. Just be sure to brush up on page layout before the interview. And talk about golf to the man. He's an avid birdie chaser. It wouldn't hurt to cackle about some minor sports if you really want to impress the guy. By the way, his name is Spec Arrington."

I got up and thanked him for the advice.

Hex shook my hand and wished me luck. "Say Kandall, how's that spunky wife of yours? You've got yourself a real prize, you know."

"I bet you don't know that she once sang at a nudist resort," I smiled.

"No, but that doesn't surprise me. I think your Tondelayo is capable of almost anything. But hell, she doesn't look anything like Hedy Lamarr."

Once more I was keenly impressed by Hex Grantham. He had thought enough about the gag to rummage through the *Clarion's* morgue to discover Tondelayo's screen identity. Still, it was Hex's faith in me that I most admired. He was using his influence to help me get started with my career, even though I was still just an unknown novice in journalistic ranks.

Nor did Hex Grantham stand on ceremony. Brig and I had not dressed up in suit and tie, spit and polish, when we first met him that night at Charlie's. We saw him, and kept seeing him as he was and where he was, a man who appreciated life in its clear, gurgling brook. For Hex, life was easily found and accepted away from grungy people with their foppish behavior. Hex used the back booth at Charlie's to find a haven, something so many people would never have sought in such a place. He shared that haven with us every time we saw him there. It was a retreat from the daily rat race across the street at *The Clarion*. That confirmed, I remembered, what the old couple at the nudist resort had said to Maydell and me

Maydell had been right when she called Hex an old softy. He might scald a lot of people with his quirky writing style, but Hex had shown us his other self, and it was thoroughly human and understandable. I hoped that quality Hex had revealed would be the mantle I wore as I moved into my career. I knew I would need it for the catapult I expected to find when I began dishing out sports culture every day for the Abilene paper.

My interview with Spec Arrington verified that. He was a man with a tumid ego that overshadowed his poor eyesight. He kept squinting at me during the interview while he prattled about the lengthy accomplishments in his life. Spec Arrington, I realized, was a perfectionist, and that bothered me. He railed about my casual attire. All his standards towered like Himalayan soil, holy ground that would surely purge any mediocre footsteps trampling on them. He informed me that's why he fired the staffer I would replace. I'll always think I got the job only because I happened to mention Ben Hogan and other golfing greats. That was my stroke of good luck even though I actually cared very little about the sport itself.

THE HELPERS

As I traveled back to Waco, I kept loathing the *Clarion* publisher's protégé. I preferred working for Hex Grantham more than ever.

Before our graduation ceremony with the class of '50, Brig joined Maydell and me at a spiffy new Italian restaurant in Waco for lunch. We raised our wine glasses as a toast to each other.

"To the families who gave us life," Maydell proposed.

"To *Alma Mater* who has broadened our scope of life," I added.

Brigdon lifted his glass with us as we spoke. Momentarily, he said nothing. He then raised his glass again in a contemplative gesture.

"To the good memory of our dear friend Freddie Foster who lost her life," he sighed.

We delicately sipped the warm red wine. In those reflective moments, I think we sensed that the wine was much like life. It was something not to be gulped down and wasted with overblown haste, but rather it was to be relished in symphony with the daily bread of Divine grace. That bread was to be chewed and digested slowly while it gave fulfillment. It was, I thought, the perfect blend in life, that of joy and necessity.

As we dined on ravioli, salad, and breadsticks, we recalled some of the campus high jinks during our Baylor years.

"The best was that January blizzard when Monday classes were canceled," Brig suggested. "We spent the day throwing snowballs at everybody---even some of the faculty."

"Yeah, and all the gals screamed as they got dumped in the snow," I laughed. "But they actually enjoyed all that attention."

"That's a lot of bull hockey, Homan Kandall," said Maydell. "I didn't like having you unbutton my shirt and touch my bra with that fistful of snow."

"But we were already engaged," I lamely responded. "Okay, how about that tug-of-war that May Day? It turned into a mud bath. I tried to save you from those barbarian rope tuggers, but I wound up in the soup with you. That was more fun than the time we made mud pies in your backyard when we were kids."

"I appreciated your feeble rescue attempt," said Maydell. "But I had to laugh when I saw all that mud caked on your face. I could tell you flinched when I told you we ought to take a shower together. But like you said, we were already engaged, so who cared a gnat's behind."

"How about the big-winning basketball team?" asked Brig. "That '48 bunch played for the national championship."

"Maybe they will again some day when Homan's there to cover the game," Maydell said.

Brig smiled and took a final sip of wine. "Why, of course. And Kandy will be seated right next to Hex Grantham in the press box."

"I would drink to that, but I don't have any more wine," I said.

"Let's refill our glasses," Maydell suggested. "Let's salute ourselves as the champions we can be for each other. Let's pledge to care and share, regardless of whatever rocks life may throw at us."

Brig leaned across the table and pecked Maydell on the cheek.

"That's from Freddie," he smiled. "She may be toasting us this very moment with a glass of some heavenly vino."

Chapter Seven
Confessions

THE COLD WAR, long a festering sore, finally hit the skillet in Korea only a month after our graduation. Communist North Korea invaded South Korea, backed by the Soviet Union and later by Red China. Hex Grantham may have missed a lot of football predictions, but he had rightly called this conflict that night when Brig and I first met him at Charlie's.

The United Nations, meaning America primarily, jumped into the fray to aid South Korea. The war was initially labeled a *police action*, but it revolved into much more than a mere sideshow conflict. It was bitterly fought for three numbing years in bits and bursts by both sides.

It seemed like a stupid war to me, coming so soon after the Second World War when the combatants had been allies. Many years later, I enjoyed the hilarious sitcom M.A.S.H. because of its zany characters, especially the medicos. With all of their ribald humor, they provided a relentless challenge to the idiocy of the war.

The Korean episode continued to unravel America.

THE HELPERS

College campuses were hotbeds for protests and political unrest. I feared the U.S. would never recover, regardless of the war's outcome.

Brigdon Chonliff hated the protests because he felt they hollowed American patriotism. He and I disagreed about re-enlisting in the Armed Forces. I was negative-minded, and Brig was gung-ho about the idea. I could not understand his readiness to serve again in the Air Force. I certainly did not want to wave my semaphore flags again. I had Maydell and her wifely presence disenchanted me about the Navy.

Brig had moved to Corpus Christi after our graduation, and true to his promise, Colonel Fredrick Foster staked him to a career in photography. Even more, he gave him a scenic house on the bayside beach. Those gifts should have meant security for Brig, but he stubbornly rejected the thought.

Colonel Foster and Brig argued when he wanted to re-enlist in the Air Force. Brig called it a patriotic duty, but the colonel ridiculed the idea of a new enlistment as pure folly.

"Look son", he said hotly, "the Air Force doesn't need both of us. I'm a career man, and I fully expect to be called to serve actively in Korea. But you're a civilian and you damn well need to remain a civilian. I've provided for your future and you've got things to take care of right here in Corpus. I want you to look after Phyllis while I'm gone.

"This town is her home, and she'll need your support. But that works both ways. She's not in favor of this war like I am. So she needs to stay out of it and help you in your new business venture. Brigdon, you're like a son to both of us, don't you see?"

Brig was not impressed with Colonel Foster's plea.

"No Colonel, I don't see. I don't see that at all. I truly appreciate all you have done for me, but you and Phyllis ought to let me get out of your lives. I'm fraudulent. I'm a chameleon, a moral misfit who can't possibly measure up to your standards as an officer and a gentleman, certainly not after I had sex with Freddie one night in Cameron Park up in Waco just before she got sick."

Brig paused, expecting outrage by Fredrick Foster, but it never surfaced.

"Sir, doesn't that shock you? It certainly should. Do I have to be crude and tell you that your daughter and I locked loins? Do I have to say the f-word to rouse your indignation?"

Colonel Foster looked at him squarely, but with a steady, benevolent smile.

"No Brigdon, you don't. That's not necessary. You see, Freddie informed us of the incident herself before she died. She told her mother and me how strong she came on to you there in the park. Freddie said she instigated the tryst and accepted sole responsibility for it. She also told us how tender you were and how loving you performed. With tears in her eyes, she said it made her proud to escape being the little mouse she had always been. Freddie wanted Phyllis and me to clearly understand that. Those were her final words to us there in the hospital."

Brig relaxed with a heavy sigh. "I truly loved her. Sir, our sex scene wasn't a sudden flight into lunacy. I want you to know that. It happened because we both wanted it to happen. Those few minutes were precious to us, something we cherished and would have always cherished, even though we knew it was wrong."

THE HELPERS

"Phyllis and I gave our daughter our parental forgiveness, and Brigdon, we likewise forgave you," Colonel Foster said. "Decent human beings must always find a way to forgive. Otherwise, the lives they lead have no more taste than a cup of vapid chicken broth. Brigdon, I'm glad you were man enough to inform me about what happened, and I want you to realize that your confession only reinforces our feelings about you. We're glad you helped Freddie have that ecstasy before she died."

Brig informed Maydell and me of the conversation in a long, rambling letter.

When the letter arrived, Maydell and I were settled in a comfortable apartment in Abilene. Not even the Kentucky Derby roses could have looked better for us. I had learned how to tolerate the snappish Spec Arrington on his sports staff, and Maydell secured a choral position in one of the city's junior high schools. We joined a prominent Methodist church because of the reputation its choir held in the city. Abilene became our home, and we enjoyed our community involvement.

Maydell became one of the contraltos in the choir. With her talent, she later won the role of *Laurie* in *Oklahoma* that was presented by the Abilene Civic Theatre. Her career zoomed with that performance. Other performances with roles as a soloist quickly followed.

The news from Brig surprised us, especially Maydell.

"Good Lord, who would have ever thought that Freddie Foster would get plugged before I did?" she whimpered.

"Bad timing, sweetheart", I teasingly said. "It was merely a stroke of bad timing. But one of these years when you're on the road to motherhood, it won't matter."

Chapter Eight
The Tender Thread

THE YEAR OF MOTHERHOOD never came for Maydell Kandall.

The Korean War ended in 1953, the year she died, three months pregnant. She was crossing the street to our church's parking lot on a Wednesday night after choir rehearsal when she was crushed by a speeding hit-and-run driver, a young Mexican national high on crack cocaine.

According to an eye witness, also a choir member, the Mexican stopped momentarily, got out and yelled something at Maydell sprawled on the street. He then raced away in a stolen car. The choir member described the man to the police who later found him asleep on a park bench near downtown Abilene. He had left the car a block away where he banged it into a street sign.

I was laying out copy for the sports section of *The Abilene Chronicle* when the night city editor rushed over to my desk with the terrible news.

"Homan, we just got a call from St. Andrew's. Get over there right now. Your wife got bashed by some idiot in front of your church when he ran over her. The hospital says she's hurt real bad. I'll have Newman put the sports section to bed for you."

When I arrived at the hospital a bespectacled nun led me into a small waiting room. She crossed herself and mumbled a prayer on my behalf.

"Thank you, Sister" I murmured. I was pacing around the room when the doctor entered.

He removed his glasses before he spoke, a symbol of regrettable news, I was sure.

"We couldn't save her, Mr. Kandall," he said flatly. "Your wife had massive internal injuries. I'm very sorry to inform you of her death."

Massive internal injuries. That's always been a catch-all phrase in newsprint. It is clear and concise, but it never fully reveals the *why* or the *how* of a person's death. And in Maydell's case, the fetus she carried in her stomach was also destroyed. In those awful moments in that hospital waiting room, I could find no balm in Gilead to soothe my rage. All I felt was a cascading surge of contempt for the young punk who had caused the death of my beloved Maydell.

I traveled to Waxahachie for her funeral. At their request, the service was held in the Collins' church. Their pastor would officiate, and Geraud, now an eighteen year old ministerial student at Baylor, would assist. The arrangements suited me fine because initially I was too numb to make any significant decisions.

Geraud returned to Waxahachie with me after he had rushed out to Abilene to help take care of some of the preliminaries with the funeral home.

"Don't you have some request for the funeral", he asked.

"I would like for it to include a eulogy. I have thought about doing a eulogy for Maydell."

"Can you do it without breaking down? Homan, I know it would not be easy for you."

My answer was decisive. "Geraud, you're right. Both you and I will be emotionally drained. But Maydell always believed that some day I would write something with the stamp of true greatness upon it. I haven't written that eloquent prose as yet, but that's what I'll be reaching for when I write that eulogy for her funeral tomorrow."

I found a deep and abiding solace knowing Brig had arrived from Corpus Christi and was present to hear it. I was also gratified that a choir soloist sang *Climb Every Mountain*. That inspirational piece of music had been Geraud's idea because he knew Maydell sang it as the Reverend Mother in a production of *The Sound Of Music*. Her musical advice in that song had captivated me, and I was thankful for Geraud's sensitivity.

My eulogy began shakily. My hands grasped both sides of the pulpit as I looked at the crowded church pews.

"I'm a sportswriter, not a philosopher," I said, trying to put firmness into my words. "But in this service for my dear wife and you family members and friends, I want to share with you some thoughts, not about death, but about life.

"Life, as I have observed it, is a tender thread. It is woven into the finest fabric God ever created, our humanity. It blends perfectly into a masterpiece designed to catch in spirit a purpose only known by Him.

"But because life is a tender thread, sometimes it becomes

THE HELPERS

pulled, or snipped, or torn loose from its base. Either by neglect, or accident, or a shameful tear, the tender thread is ruined. There are, of course, people who wish it could be restored, woven back into life. But that thread, that life, can never be humanly restored. It has been snuffed out, and only a loving God can fashion that broken thread into a new fabric called eternal life.

"For our lovely and vivacious Maydell, the thread was ripped apart by a shameless individual caught in the quagmire of drug abuse. He now awaits a courtroom trial.

"And for us who are gathered in this church, we continue to wait for our grief to subside. In time, it must. But Maydell, whose body we see in her open casket, no longer awaits entrance into the Divine, eternal kingdom. We rejoice that she has already achieved that status. We smile through our tears because she has taken her lovely trained voice with her to join a heavenly chorus. And if piccolos are played up there in the Pearly Gate Band, I surely think Maydell will be assigned First Chair in the seating arrangement."

Again I had to brace myself behind the pulpit.

"What then, is mortal life all about? Well, it's more than sports. It's more than the New York Yankee pin stripe, more than the World Series, or UT versus OU, or Ohio State versus Michigan, or any football rivalry. Life is more than the Masters, or Wimbledon, or the Triple Crown in horse racing, or anything else that takes a bow on any sports page.

"Life is also more than winning big on some game show. It is more than political parties, whatever preference a person may have. Life is more than a nightly dose of outlandish sitcoms, or even seeing the imposing Grand Canyon which

Maydell and I did. If life does not mean more than any of those things, it is void. It lacks an inner spirit in those people who would settle for the lesser things in life at the expense of revealing their finer, imaginative selves to the world as a showcase of the Almighty."

My words seemed to mesmerize the congregation. I had more to say about Maydell, but I did not want to prolong the funeral.

"In that endeavor, Maydell did not waste her short life as a daughter, sister, niece, a college grad, or as my wife. She had a motto---*Caring is Sharing*, and that's how she always conducted herself. With that gracious heart, Maydell climbed every mountain, forded every stream, and followed every rainbow to find a dream that required all the love she could give every day of her life, and she gave that love generously in fulfillment of that dream.

"And now I will say goodbye to her with the words of a song that became our favorite: *I'll be seeing you in all the old familiar places that this heart of mine embraces all day through. I'll find you in the morning sun.* Yes, my darling, in the morning sun, I'll find you somewhere and I'll see you again."

My eyes were visibly damp as I moved away from the pulpit. Geraud came to my side and hugged me with florid compassion.

"I saw Maydell undressed that time when I was a little kid," he whispered. "But you have seen her clothed in a flowing celestial gown called the abundant life. Thanks for that inspiring tribute to my sister, good buddy."

At the cemetery Brig and I moved away from the throng of people after the benediction. Friends and family alike were hesitant to leave, but they somehow noticed that Brig and I needed to talk privately. Given that courtesy, we were not interrupted.

"How are you going to cope with this?" he asked.

"I'll keep Maydell's piccolo, like you did with Freddie's."

"Kandy, you will need to do more than that. You will need to find some forgiveness for that hophead who's in jail for what he did."

"I hope he rots there. That's what he deserves."

"Maybe so, but he's one of those tender threads you talked about in the eulogy."

"He's nothing but goddamned Mexican dog shit," I retorted mordantly. I looked over my shoulder, hoping none of the onlookers heard my outburst of profanity.

"Just remember this, Kandy. The Fosters forgave Freddie and me. That wasn't easy for them. Forgiveness has a very hard exterior to crack, but it can be accomplished."

I tried to change the subject. "How is Colonel Foster these days? Still hacked because he didn't get to Korea?"

"He's fine, and he and Phyllis send their condolences to you. He is even willing to forgive Harry Truman for kicking MacArthur's ass over there."

"Well, sooner or later, there's bound to be another nice mess somewhere. That's what Oliver Hardy was always saying to Stan Laurel. . .another nice mess. Maybe Truman will have the opportunity to do some more ass-kicking."

Brig grabbed me by the arm. "Kandy, just don't kick yourself in the tush. Find some compassion, even a nickel's worth, for that doped up Mexican."

At last people started leaving the burial site when the

funeral attendants ushered the Collins and my parents off to the company limo. Two of Maydell's Baylor classmates came by and congratulated me for the eulogy.

Thankfully, they mentioned nothing about forgiveness.

I appreciated that omission. The subject of forgiveness was strictly taboo, the way my anger had gushed out against Maydell's killer, Alonzo Perieda. That hostility now extended to all Hispanics, even Julio and Choya Fuentes, those good American citizens with the Christmas Eve tamales.

Chapter Nine
Lo Siento

PERIEDA'S TRIAL was held in an Abilene courtroom, despite a change of venue request. It had been sought by the youthful looking court-appointed defense attorney, a sharp grad from the University of Texas Law School named Ted Dossler.

He had his client well-dressed and clean shaven during the three day trial. That was a ploy, of course. He wanted people in the courtroom to be impressed by Alonzo Perieda's appearance and render their sympathy to the young man.

I was not that lenient minded. I sat next to the prosecuting attorney in that packed courtroom, and I began staring relentlessly at Perieda the moment the trial started.

Ted Dossler noticed my contempt, and quickly complained to the judge that I was harassing his client. His Honor agreed and warned me to shift my eyes away from the defendant.

I reluctantly complied, but that did not alter my bitter feelings about Perieda.

Since Perieda understood little if any English, a translator sat beside him during the trial, conversing with him in Spanish.

The trial hinged largely on the testimony of the choir member who witnessed the crime, an elderly gentleman named Morgan. He testified that Perieda came careening through the church parking lot and into the street Maydell was crossing. He then deliberately slammed the car into Maydell who had no chance to dodge its impact. Mr. Morgan, a square jawed man, described in gripping detail how Maydell was knocked to the pavement. He also told the court how Perieda jumped out of the car and yelled something at her before he fled down the street.

"Mr. Morgan, what did the defendant yell at the victim, Mrs. Kandall?" the prosecutor asked.

"What he said to her was in Spanish. But I understand Spanish quite fluently. I taught it at McMurry here in Abilene before my retirement."

"What in Spanish did he say?"

"The defendant said, 'You bitch, you should have stayed out of my way.'"

That statement caused a loud murmur among the spectators.

The prosecutor asked the translator, a slim young woman with coppery hair, to repeat those words in Spanish.

She did so with some hesitancy. She obviously did not like to say the Spanish version of the b-word.

"And that's what you heard the defendant say to Mrs. Kandall?" the prosecutor questioned.

"That's exactly what he said."

Ted Dossler jumped to his feet. "Objection", he cried out.

"Lots of people use that word. It has become a common word. People don't mean it literally. It's just an expression my client unwisely used in a moment of stress. The prosecution cannot show the defendant said the word with malice. Nor can it be shown that Mrs. Kandall's death was anything more than an accident. It was a dreadful accident, but that's all that it was."

"Sustained", the judge answered. "The testimony presented does not reveal any clear intent by the defendant to degrade the victim, Mrs. Kandall."

The prosecutor, a tall man with a hawkish face, continued his interrogation.

"Mr. Morgan, why did you concentrate your attention on the defendant? You saw Mrs. Kandall crumpled on the street, badly hurt. Surely your first impulse would have been to render aid to her, and not be concerned about who the driver was, or what he spoke to her. Maydell Kandall was a friend, a fellow choir member. Why didn't you rush to her and provide first aid?"

The witness stirred as he turned his face toward Alonzo Perieda.

"I was the first choir member to follow Maydell Kandall out to the street. I yelled for her to look out when I saw the car, but it was too late. I knew at that moment there was nothing I could do for her, even though I was terribly concerned about what had happened. So were the other choir members who then approached. All of us loved her. But I felt it was absolutely essential that I got close enough to the defendant to identify him as the man who willfully struck her down. I had to do that on her behalf. It was my civic duty, I believe, and that's how I responded."

The young defense attorney focused his short cross examination on Mr. Morgan's age and possible hearing loss. He then quizzed him hard about the reliability of his civic duty, citing his relationship to Maydell.

"Mr. Morgan, I appreciate your civic mindedness, but please tell the court what you said to your fellow choir members when they joined you there in the street where Mrs. Kandall lay, her life ebbing away."

"I don't recall what I said."

"Must I refresh your memory for you? You made a derogatory remark about Mr. Pereida, and you laced it with expletives. Tell me, sir, how you could be so adept at recalling what Mr. Perieda said, but now you can't remember what you said about him."

Mr. Morgan squirmed in the witness chair. He looked at the prosecutor, obviously hoping for an objection.. It came, but the judge overruled it. He advised Morgan to answer the question.

He mumbled his reply, but Ted Dossler was not satisfied. "Sir, please speak up so everyone can hear."

"At the scene I called the defendant a blankety-blank *greaser.*"

"Thank you. Now sir, is it not possible that you've stretched your testimony quite a bit to strengthen the case against Mr. Perieda because he is Hispanic? Are you quite sure you saw him deliberately ram the car into Mrs. Kandall? Or is that merely what you wanted to see?"

"I'm not lying, if that's what you mean."

"Yes, sir, that's exactly what I do mean. Let me remind you that you did not retire as you stated. You were fired from

THE HELPERS

the McMurry faculty because you stated publicly at the university that you despised Hispanics even when you taught their language. Is that not true?"

"It's true," Morgan acknowledged in a shaky, terse reply. "But what I said about Hispanics came after a very bad incident involving a Mexican student."

"Please tell the court what that incident was."

Morgan completely lost his composure. "That student raped my granddaughter," he shouted. "That's why I loathe all Hispanics. They're dirt bags. You can't trust them. They don't belong in this country."

That ended the cross examination on a high note for the defense. I eyed the prosecutor with a sudden, queasy feeling about the trial. What had appeared to be an open and shut second degree murder case against Alonzo Perieda now looked like it was sinking in quicksand.

Ted Dossler was smiling broadly when he conferred briefly with Perieda and the translator following the Morgan outburst. He knew he had punched a gaping hole in the prosecution's case. It was a promising start for him as a defense attorney.

But then came the shocking, unforeseen bombshell. Alonzo Perieda surprisingly shook his head and whispered something in return. That gesture produced a momentary conversation between Dossler and the translator. The attorney abruptly questioned his client, apparently because of what Perieda had told him. Whatever Perieda said, it relaxed his grim face. He then nodded pointedly in affirmation to the question Dossler had posed.

In open dismay, Dossler finally arose from the hasty and prolonged conference, and spoke directly to the judge.

"Your Honor, if it please the court, Mr. Perieda wishes, first of all, to apologize for calling Mrs. Kandall a bitch. He refutes the idea it was a careless slip of the tongue at the scene of the crime. And he further states that it was a crime, not an accident. He wants the court to understand that he intentionally steered the car into Mrs. Kandall to maim or cripple her because she was an Anglo, an enemy."

Perieda said something else to the translator who relayed the information to Dossler.

A few moments later Dossler had additional remarks for the judge.

"Your Honor, my client has informed me that when he drifted into this town, he hoped to become a legal citizen and be useful. But he couldn't shake his drug habit, and people loathed him because of it. No one tried to help him. Then in his drug-induced rage, he just craved to maim someone, anyone who happened to get in his way. It was his act of revenge against an uncaring society."

The translator furnished another bit of information to Dossler from Perieda.

"Now my client wants the court to know he's very sorry he killed the lady, especially when he learned she was pregnant. But he also says that if it had not been her, he would have deliberately targeted someone else. Mr. Perieda therefore asks that his plea be changed to guilty, and he throws himself at the mercy of the court. He is asking this because he does not want to prolong the trial, nor the grief of Mr. Kandall and his friends."

The judge ordered a recess and asked both attorneys to come to his chambers. That surely meant some major decision

THE HELPERS

would be reached affecting the outcome of the trial. I still believed that regardless of Perieda's confession, he merited a very long stay behind prison bars. What baffled me was the *why* of his abrupt request. Perhaps Brig was right when he reminded me that Alonzo Perieda was indeed a tender thread. I sat there blankly trying to decide.

After the recess, the startling developments ended with an adjournment, and the second day of the trial was over. Alonzo Perieda was led out of the courtroom. He passed by within my earshot. Halting for a brief moment, he turned toward me and spoke softly in Spanish.

"*Lo siento,*" he murmured.

I asked the translator what the words meant. She answered my question with a nonchalant shrug.

"Mr. Kandall, he said *I'm sorry.*"

I pondered her reply as I left the courtroom. I wondered if Alonzo Perieda was truly sorry about anything. I found myself unwilling to place any truth in the two words he said to me. His admission of guilt did not soften my feelings about the guy one stingy bit. He was to blame for Maydell's death, not the society that ignored him.

The jury deliberated that night. The next morning it quickly rendered its guilty verdict to the court. Alonzo Perieda accepted the verdict with no emotion. He slumped into his chair, staring calmly at the floor.

The prosecutor told me he and Dossler approved the judge's suggestion that with the guilty plea, he would reduce the charge to aggravated manslaughter and impose a lighter prison sentence.

"Is that suitable with you, Mr. Kandall?"

I kept gazing at Perida, this time without any judicial restraint. As I did, I remembered what Brig had said about a nickel's worth of forgiveness. Even more pungent were the words of Colonel Foster that Brig quoted in his long and substantive letter about the sex he and Freddie had in Cameron Park.

Decent human beings must always find a way to forgive. Otherwise, the lives they lead have no more appeal than a cup of vapid chicken broth.

In serious contemplation, I rested my chin in the palm of my hand. I knew then my own life had to amount to something better than vapid chicken broth. Only after that resolution did I answer the prosecuting attorney.

"Yes, it is," I said firmly.

As Alonzo Perieda was led out of the courtroom to begin serving his prison sentence with no possible parole for five years, I once more glared at him, but this time with genuine pity. He truly was another *tender thread*.

"Lo siento," I said as he passed by wearing handcuffs.

I wanted to believe he understood that I spoke those words, not in derision, but as a true measure of sympathy.

Before I left the courtroom I spoke briefly with Ted Dossler. I knew he was unhappy with his client's drastic confession.

"Please tell me why you think Alonzo Perieda changed his plea after you stymied the prosecution," I said.

"Mr. Kandall, I wish I knew. I had something going for him, but I guess conscience intervened. How could I compete against that colossus of the human mind? Conscience only has one standing rule for which it can validate itself. It ultimately has to be clear and squeaky clean, and that's the way Alfonzo Perieda chose to respond."

With my own conscience now clear, that night I called Brigdon in Corpus Christi. "Brig," I said, "I'm coping the way you suggested."

"Kandy, that's great to hear. Now get back to work. You've got a lot of writing to do before you overtake Grantland Rice."

Chapter Ten
Little Jack Horner

THE YEARS THAT FOLLOWED were mercurial in Brigdon's career and mine.

Chonliff Photography became a buzz word in the Corpus Christi business community. His studio was a big money-maker, but Brig preferred to free lance. He snapped pictures of anything that captured his delight, but he especially loved the coastal waters and ships of all shapes and sizes. They included anything from the old aircraft carrier, the USS Lexington that rested in the bay, to shrimp boats and yachts. In moments of pure escape, Brig photographed bikini-clad girls twisting their bottoms while they strolled along the beach of North Padre Island.

I was the recipient of those photos that included a caption that usually read something like *As you can see, the fishing is great down here.*

But it was those pictures of the Lexington that I admired the most. True, they brought back those bitter memories of the Yorktown during the battle at Midway, but those memories no longer tormented my mind. This old Navy vet

THE HELPERS

had survived that aftermath of the war, and I viewed the Lexington as a symbol of personal strength and durability. I hoped the tourists who climbed aboard the ship had the same feeling.

Brig also sent numerous pictures of his bay front home. He called it *The Beachcomber,* and it seemed to me that he was always adding new features to it. The house was already too large for Brig, who like myself, was creeping into middle age. *The Beachcomber* was a two-tiered rambling house with a backyard that sloped down to the shoreline where he erected a cabana. Brig decorated the interior of his home with pictures and bric-a-brac that spoke of the lure sea-faring men had for its deep, dark waters.

"Get down here and see for yourself," he once told me in a phone conversation. "It will remind you of that old movie you loved so much, *Reap The Wild Wind.*"

"It was Paulette Goddard that I loved---her and Raymond Massey, the villain," I laughed.

That phone chat ended with another of my periodic pledges to come down and guest at *The Beachcomber. Someday, at least by the twenty-first century.*

I truly wanted to see Brig and spend some time with him, but my own career was now at its pinnacle. I became sports editor of *The Abilene Chronicle* two years after Maydell's death. Spec Arrington retired and handed me the reins, with a compliment for never bowing to his whimsical ego.

"Homan," he said, 'you've earned this promotion. I'm just sorry that you were Hex Grantham's disciple and not mine. That old sourpuss finally excelled as a sportswriter when he sent you out here. I'm very thankful that he did."

The paper and the people of Abilene liked my style and the coverage I gave their favorite teams, including the new second high school in the city.

In 1980 I was elected to the Texas Sportswriters Hall of Fame. The ceremonial banquet was held at the convention center in Waco where I had Brig and Geraud Collins as my guests. During my acceptance speech I had a singular word about Hex Grantham.

"I only wish Hex was still alive and present here tonight. He was my mentor all through my Baylor years and beyond. Hex, by his example, taught me that you are a person first, a unique individual, and that placing halos on sports is secondary. He showed me that what you write is only important if you have a passion for it and yourself, and for the people who play their crazy games."

But those years also revealed that, despite fame and a hefty bank balance, life also has its shallows that people wade in continually. Those shallows are all right for gigging flounders in bay waters, but life remains incomplete if people never venture out into the depths.

Brig and I knew that essentially we had settled for flounders. We were two lonely men who were aging without the adhesive tape of feminine companionship and sexual gratification. Our career achievements were the only thing holding us together for the long haul into our senior years---that and a Lazy Susan that spun pill bottles around to us each day. Without a woman's care and affection, we were already limping along, even though our masculine pride still claimed we had a clanging zest for living.

Both of us began to realize that claim was an odious falsehood.

THE HELPERS

True enough, we still kept the two piccolos Maydell and Freddie had once played. But for what purpose, we did not know. Those instruments had become mere artifacts that no longer linked us to our women except during the restless heaves of nostalgia. Thus in reality, those piccolos were becoming relics like Brigdon Chonliff and Homan Kandall. They weren't loved. They weren't tuned, and they weren't played. And that became a heavy coating of dust that nullified their value.

One year at a Baylor homecoming I spotted Geraud Collins in the Student Union Building. The little pest who had tagged along with Maydell and me to a couple of movies was now a prominent Baptist preacher in East Texas. He was an imposing figure, tall and broad-shouldered. He was wearing a green suit with a gold shirt and a striped necktie. Geraud looked rather pompous, but he squeezed my hand in a vice-like clamp as a gesture of renewing our friendship. We sat down and had a cup of coffee.

"It's too bad that we don't have any hot tamales to peel, good buddy," he chuckled.

As we exchanged information about ourselves, I told him I still had Maydell's piccolo. "Can you find some use for it?" I asked.

Geraud shook his head rather sullenly.

"I'm afraid not, Homan. My three kids are hooked on space. They want to blast off skyward in one of those silver chariots and explore the wild unknown. They don't have an ounce of musical talent among them. None at all, and that's sad, a very sad blank in a Baptist parsonage."

"My friend Brigdon Chonliff still has his girlfriend's

piccolo. Those little tweeters are absolutely useless to us, except to pamper our nostalgia. I suppose that nostalgia is why we never offered the piccolos to any school or charity."

"Then by heaven, find someone to play them," said Geraud. "You and Brigdon need to find someone who can add some music to your lives. Don't be a couple of ninnies for the rest of your days---and nights. Do you remember what Jesus said to his fishing chums who had labored all night there in the lake, but had caught nothing? He told them to ease out into the deep water, let down their nets, and then they would haul up a mess of fish. Homan, that's what you and your friend Brigdon need to do."

I smiled at his comparison. "Brig and I aren't fishing for anything, women or whatever, if that's what you mean. We have good lives. We have some wonderful memories we share with each other."

Geraud took a final sip of his coffee.

"That's the trouble with you Methodists, Homan. Your church is in trouble, but it's coasting along, just resting on the memories of its heyday. You have no new John Wesley to prod you into greater accomplishments. But good buddy, that's true of a lot of churches, including my Baptist beloveds. Mainline denominations are beginning to feel the apathy of their members. That's a pinch of the venom the Vietnam war has heaped on people everywhere in its aftermath."

I felt like I was hearing a good Baptist sermon.

"Change is becoming dominant," Geraud declared, "and it's unacceptable to many hard hats. So they back away from the consequences and become like Little Jack Horner. You remember that Mother Goose stalwart, don't you?"

THE HELPERS

"He was one of my early heroes."

"Well, you know then that he sat in a corner eating his Christmas pie. He stuck in his thumb and pulled out a plum, and gloated, *what a good boy am I*. People like him settle for similar minor triumphs. They aren't willing to stick their thumbs into something challenging, something with a high reward potential. They are content with the same old Christmas pie. That's complacency, and it is hideous. Good buddy, I think that has affected you, I'm sorry to say. But this is homecoming, so let's say with all the old grads, sic 'em, Bears."

I finished my coffee and placed the cup in the saucer. "Geraud, you're quite a preacher. Maydell would be awfully proud of you."

He smiled. It was a warm, cheery smile, the kind he surely bestowed on his congregation every Sunday. But just then I was thankful that I had him to myself, even for those few minutes we had shared. Now a lot Baylor exes were streaming into the Student Union lobby, and I knew Geraud must bound off to spread homecoming cheer with them. I just wished Geraud Collins was a Methodist, perhaps the new John Wesley he had mentioned. He would challenge me thoroughly, I knew, to break loose from the stale, old Christmas pie I kept thumbing with such ineffectual results.

On Sunday night I called Brig. He asked me about the homecoming hoopla.

"You should have been there. It was great. I heard a Mother Goose rhyme."

Brig replied through his laughter. "Okay, I want to hear about it. You can tell me while we sit on our round mounds out on the top deck down here and sip mint juleps like good Southern gentlemen have always done."

"Better still, we could learn to play those piccolos and pipe away our lonely nights."

"Kandy, what we really need are a couple of dancing girls with a come hither look in their moonbeam eyes."

"Okay, you find them. Then I'll coming running."

When I spoke those words, I never dreamed such a capricious remark would ever emerge from absurdity into fact.

Chapter Eleven
Goodbye, Grantland Rice

I RETIRED from the *Abilene Chronicle* ten years later in1990 at the summit of my career. Within those years I had offers to bring my talents to newspapers in much larger cities, but I always declined. Abilene was where Maydell and I had lived, and it was there that I wanted to remember her both in life and death. It was a memory flirtation that I chose not to break.

During that career walk in the sun, I achieved high acclaim for the devotion I gave to sports. I spoke at high school banquets and contributed articles to the highly successful *Texas Football* magazine. At various times I covered NFL games involving the Dallas Cowboys. I did numerous interviews with college and pro players including Don Meredith when he heckled the opinionated Howard Cosell on the *Monday Night Football* telecasts for ABC. I chummed with Hall of Famers, and I covered a World Series one year. In another year, I did a spread on the Final Four in college basketball for the *New York Times*.

Before I retired, I wrote a book about the sports legends

Texas had produced. It became an immediate best-seller. I knew then I had everything a sports jockey could possibly desire. *Except genuine happiness*, that is. Without Maydell, happiness still eluded me.

Brig begged me to scuttle my retirement plans during a long phone conversation.

"Kandy, you can't quit now. You're hot on the heels of Grantland Rice. He's a legend, but you're ready to eclipse him. You're the now. Grantland Rice is history."

My argument with Brig was stern and stiff.

"Look, there are a lot of greats in my profession. I'll let them ascend up Mount Olympus and seek Grantland Rice's throne. I just want to spend the next few years writing something rather than sports."

"You need to do what you do best, my friend," he replied.

"Brig, I'm nearly 65 years old. I've lost my passion for sports. I've grown weary of the claptrap trend sports have taken, especially football. Now we've got college teams trying to ape their NFL big brothers. TV has become a fierce, devouring monster that shovels out huge bounty to schools willing to sell their souls in exchange for a place in the limelight of TV screens. That monster has become the golden god of college football all across the country. Look at SMU. The NCAA kicked the school into oblivion because it cheated hot and heavy while trying to quick-step its way on the yellow brick road to gridiron glory."

"So there are some bad apples in college football. Kandy, that shouldn't turn all sports into castor oil."

"Brig, I wish that were true. But you're overlooking how college and NBA basketball have been scandalized by the

THE HELPERS

druggies and point-shavers who have slam-dunked the sport. The public eye doesn't give a popcorn fart about that, however. It only focuses upon its heroes in baggy shorts who give people the cheers they need to forget the American groundswell of decadence."

My momentary pause gave Brig the chance to regroup.

"Man, that's quite a soap box you're on," he said.

"Yeah, I guess it is, and I haven't even mentioned the millionaire boys of summer. With their high price tag salaries and free agent access, they don't care if the fans get their butts numbed by those World Series night games up north in a season that stretches almost into November, thanks to the moguls who are in cahoots with the TV beast."

The conversation with Brigdon did not collapse on that sour note, but I now realized that neither he nor anyone else could change my mind about retiring.

So best said, the day that I cleaned out my desk at *The Abilene Chronicle* and departed was right for me and the newspaper. I had become too controversial, even more than Hex Grantham had ever been. I said goodbye to the city room staff in a nice farewell party they arranged, and I thanked each one for their journalistic juice that kept the paper flowing every day.

But those dedicated staffers knew, as I knew, that newspapers, like mainline churches, were suffering. Readership continued to dwindle because the printed page no longer had any brisk appeal. The catchy style of TV cameras and commentators had captive audiences that enjoyed the news events, sordid, nasty, and bloody, whenever they happened. Nor could newspaper ads compete with the raucous stuff that splattered TV screens. Many daily papers, even *The Houston Post*, had already succumbed to the blitz of the major networks, and I feared other papers were digging their reportorial graves as well.

The last thing I grabbed off my desk was a picture of Maydell. I still hoped, after the long crunch of time, to see her somewhere on some copious morning with the mirth of sunshine splashing through her hair.

I returned to Waxahachie for a short, sentimental visit. On a damp, rainy afternoon I went to the cemetery where Maydell was buried. I stood beside her grave as raindrops pelted my dark hat. Out of deference, I removed it and hummed our song.

"Sweetheart, today is not like that lovely summer day we always pictured. Nor is it bright and gay, but I will always think of you in that way. And I will find you some morning, somewhere, even in some unfamiliar place."

I moved to Waco the following week. It was now where I wanted to spend the rest of my life. Like Freddie Foster, I wanted to be close to Baylor. I devoutly hoped the old school would offer me at least few grams of renewal.

The university had long ceased to be a snug little territorial outpost for higher education in South Waco. Its enrollment had almost tripled since Brigdon Chonliff and I trudged around the campus. Several new buildings now graced the landscape, including a swank, breath-taking Communications edifice, and others were under construction.

The campus was abuzz with activity the day I drove by. Pat Neff, a former Texas governor, had kept the school afloat during the Great Depression as its president. He would have been amazed, and perhaps shocked, to see how Baylor had grown. And probably Neff would have been chagrined to see coeds moving about, clad in shorts and sandals that revealed their painted toenails. A lot of old rules he had crafted no longer applied. Baylor University was now firmly entrenched in the 20th century, and to me it looked like a good fit. *Alma mater* was atwitter over its future and justly so, I thought.

I smiled broadly as I moved along. Old Baylor and an aging Homan Kandall were linked together again.

Continuing my route on South Fifth Street, I drove out to the Oakwood Cemetery. With some difficulty, I found Freddie Foster's tombstone. I remained there for a few moments admiring the beauty of the sturdy oak trees that clustered the cemetery, so restful and serene in its dignity.

In one of the trees, I spotted a robin that chirped its salute to life. I vowed I would inform Brig that the remains of his own little robin were safe and secure underneath that small patch of God's good earth.

Chapter Twelve
No Stinkin' Bodges

I BECAME ANTSY to write a new book, not fiction, but something aloof from the glitzy atmosphere of sports.

Being an old movie buff who could rattle off the names of countless character actors and actresses now gone, I wanted to bring them back to life on the printed page. Those people, I felt, deserved that kind of recognition for what they contributed to the golden era of Hollywood. *They also made a telling contribution to society,* I told myself. *They never became involved in movieland scandals.*

They had supporting movie roles like so many people in real life. They knew their range in comedy or drama, and they found satisfaction in being a helpful part of someone else's life. They never achieved star billing, but they helped bring stardom to the Hollywood greats. And perhaps best of all, those people were easy to identify. Movie audiences saw them over and over again and recognized them every time they saw them on the screen, maybe not by name, but certainly by their faces and the roles they played.

THE HELPERS

I felt the new breed of supporting actors and actresses, largely unknown, could never supplant a Henry Travers or a Hattie McDaniel, a Thomas Mitchell or a Beulah Bondi, a Franklin Pangborn or a Willie Best, or the jowly and loveable S.Z. Sakall, affectionately known as *Cuddles*. I even wanted to include the famous Max Steiner whose movie musical scores always gave me a lot of spine tingles.

Of course I sensed a certain risk about the book. Many persons were saliently sports-minded. They wanted to read about their champions, not about old movie has-beens, virtually unknown to them. I knew I would have to sell my publisher on the idea that movies were like sports teams. Not everyone was the star, but there was a vital teamwork involved in both athletics and movies.

My publisher offered a very sensible suggestion. He thought the book would have added sales appeal were I to make some of those character actors highly viable by acknowledging their roles in outstanding sports movies like *Pride Of The Yankees*. With it in mind, he quickly offered Walter Brennan as a prime candidate for the book.

Such a ploy would keep me dabbling in sports for awhile, but I easily warmed up to his idea.

"Oh yes, and there's also John Qualen who played Knute Rockne's father in that epic about Notre Dame football," I smiled. "And William Bendix played Babe Ruth. Or how about Paul Douglas who was a sports announcer before Hollywood claimed him?"

"Save your recital for the book, Homan," my publisher said. "What do you want to call this venture?"

"How about *Those Old Backup Guys?* They weren't subs.

They weren't bench warmers. They backed up the front liners and made good things happen."

He liked the football connotation and told me to get busy to meet a publication date he had in mind.

With the *Internet* came computers that made typewriters obsolete. I hated to junk my aged Smith Corona, the Christmas present from Maydell, but I had to accept progress. Once I learned how to cope with computer trickery, I quit fuming about its relentless demands. I adjusted to its quirks and began to appreciate the beauty of word processors that made writing so much easier.

The new book endeavor caused me to cancel another promise to visit *The Beachcomber*. I worked long hours researching and piecing the manuscript together to meet my deadline. Brig, now a computer whiz, accepted my excuse when I finally had a little time to correspond with him by email after *Those Old Backup Guys* went to the printer.

That brought us together again as we shared our joys and our woes. Brig sent me numerous electronic pictures of his home, himself, and the daily bustle of the Corpus Christi Bay. They helped cheer up those lonely days of my second retirement.

In return, I wrote him detailed data about many of those Hollywood gems I kept seeing on TCM during the siege of my solitary nights. As usual, I praised numerous supporting cast members I had to leave out of my new book. I often stumped Brig with their names.

On one occasion, he answered my latest email with a question. "Who played Gatewood, the banker, in that old John Wayne movie, *Stagecoach?*"

I responded immediately. "Berton Churchill."

But for once Brig had the last word. "Was he any kin to Winston?"

We loved to josh each other like that. Such good-natured email banter gave us both a boost that helped humor our advancing age. We were, in short, caring and sharing with each other. Those emails shoved aside our usual doldrums, at least temporarily.

We also talked about Baylor. We agreed to attend Homecoming in 2000 because it would mark fifty years since our graduation. We vowed we would make the scene and show all the undergrads that we were still cruising in the fast lane. It was self-deceit, of course, but it was a little candle we did not want to snuff out.

"Got any ideas how we can pull off the caper?" I wrote.

Brig furnished one that was absolutely salacious.

"We could flirt obscenely with sexy-looking coeds," he replied.

"That could cause a problem," I answered. "They might have some flirty thoughts themselves. That could be risky. Those sweeties could make us sound like a couple of old dangling participles."

"A good point," Brig responded. "Well, suppose we just learn how to play our piccolos and toot them in the homecoming parade. How'd that be for a little showmanship?"

I ignored his suggestion in my next email. I thought it much too gross to consdier. It would be a long parade, much too long for our old arthritic knees.

One of Brig's favorite email topics was about how he kept upgrading his house. He now had an indoor swimming pool that required maintenance, in addition to a lot of yard work he could not handle by himself. He was also installing running lights, red and green, atop the sides of the second story of *The Beachcomber*.

"This will give the place a true nautical look," he wrote. "Kandy, as an old Navy man, I know you will appreciate those new lights. That is, if you ever come down for a visit."

Once more, I promised that I would.

But until recently, Brig had not informed me that he made the home improvements on behalf of the Fosters. He had them come and reside with him in their senior years. Brig said he wanted to honor them that way before they finally had to move to a nursing home.

It was then that I realized, more than ever, that Brigdon Chonliff was more than a special friend. He was also a unique, loving person who had devoted himself to the care and keeping of Fredrick and Phyllis Foster. His act of kindness had not been mandatory. Acts of love are seldom, if ever mandatory. They simply form and swell on their own like an incoming tide that must show its force with relentless waves. Is it too audacious or hokey then, to say that love will always make its splash? I think not.

But I was just being my usual philosophical self. That severely irritated me. My good thoughts never seemed to get off the bench and into the game. After Maydell died, I had never found, or even sought, someone else to love.

Once again Brig added a new twist to his letters.

He talked about the people who worked for him at *The Beachcomber*. They were day laborers, handymen he called *helpers*. All were Hispanics and all of them lacked any staying

THE HELPERS

power for the jobs Brig assigned and supervised. Their defects were varied and provided grains of humor, but so ridiculous that they painted a grim side of life the helpers had in common.

Enrique was the first to come along. Brig found him at a mission station in downtown Corpus one morning after Enrique got so stoned that he came to the center the night before without any trousers. He came to work for a couple of days before saying he had a medical appointment the next day. Brig never saw him again.

Pablo was a good worker, but he told Brig because his wife, a captain in the Mexican army, was being transferred to Baja California, he no choice but to follow her there.

I offered Brig my sympathy in an email.

"Well, good help is hard to find these days. But cheer up. There are lots of illegal Mexicans pouring into Texas. Sooner or later, you will find the right guy."

Luiz became the next helper. He showed up when the running lights were being installed. According to Brig, the man was a good electrician but he frequently dozed off into *siestas* trying to sleep off beer busts the night before. After a week's work, he took his pay and disappeared.

Pedro was the most dependable worker of the lot, Brig acknowledged. But he had the bad habit of sneaking food out of the freezer in Brig's utility room.. He took the food home when he finished work each day. When Brig discovered the thefts, Pedro told him his family lived in a shantytown shack area of Corpus and never had enough to eat.

One afternoon Brig gave Pedro two sacks of groceries and drove him to the shantytown. But Pedro could not find his house even after Brig cruised past clumps of shabby dwellings for half an hour. He let Pedro keep the groceries but left him at a blighted little park on the street where the pitiful neighborhood began.

"Why don't you hire skilled workers, dependable people with good credentials?" I wrote back when I read the Pedro chapter of Brig's stories about his so-called *helpers*.

He fired back a hasty answer. "If I did that, I would be working for them. They would call the shots. They would be in control. I would have to adjust to their schedule whims, and that would monkey wrench my time. Besides that, I would lose contact with that part of the human race I see all too often, those people who shuffle along through life in their hangdog way. That bothers me. I've tried to be benevolent, hoping to change them, but I'm still batting zero."

Knowing Brigdon Chonliff, that sounded plausible enough to me. He never mentioned any deadbeats again, and I assumed the saga of the sad sack hirelings and their fracas lifestyle had ended. He and I resumed some of our email exchanges with banter about my *Those Old Backup Guys*.

I told him how I wished I had been able to weave Alfonso Bedoya into my book. Brig remembered that Bedoya had played the Mexican bandit leader in the classic movie, *The Treasure Of The Sierra Madre*. In a famous scene Bedoya told Humphrey Bogart and Walter Huston he was a Mexican military officer.

When they asked to see his badge, he replied, *"Bodges? We got no bodges. We don't have to show you no stinkin' bodges."* His broken English was perfect for the scene.

It was a great line of dialogue in a great movie. Those

words Alfonso Bedoya spoke seemed so true to life. Lots of people have no badges to identify themselves. They pretend to be someone they are not. I habitually saw myself as one of those persons. I was a lonely old spook trying to con myself into believing I had a good, radiant life.

Within the context of that movie scene, I smilingly pictured Alfonso Bedoya in a real life role as one of Brig's infamous helpers. But happily, I saw him again in the movie, *The Big Country*. This time he was a ranch hand, a good guy named Ramon who rode off into the sunset with Gregory Peck and Jean Simmons.

That final scene made me wonder if Brig and I would ever have someone to ride with us into our sunset. I thought the possibilities of that happening were indeed slight and nil.

Chapter Thirteen
I Am Tondelayo

THINGS DRASTICALLY CHANGED for Brigdon and me in 1997.

Early on a morning marred by the portent of slushy freezing rain, I relaxed at my apartment desk. I had just returned from breakfast at *Denny's* and a cheery conversation with Marie, the senior waitress and assistant manager at the restaurant. She was a woman forty something in age, a short-haired blonde who looked good in her starched uniform, a fact Marie made sure that I noticed every morning. As my personal waitress, I always left a generous tip for her in my usual booth. She was a widow who appreciated my generosity, and for that courtesy I was truly a member of that segment of society known as the *good old boys*.

On that particular morning Marie had a pertinent suggestion for me when I finished my meal with a second cup of coffee.

"Honey, you ought to get married. You look like a big ball of cat litter every morning when you come in here."

THE HELPERS

"Thanks, I'll take your proposal into fervent consideration," I laughed.

"Maybe you should. I could do more for you than serve you scrambled eggs, sausage, and hash browns for breakfast, you ought to know."

"And at night?"

"I could take of that too," she said, giving me a broad, flirty wink.

While I sat at my desk smiling about my conversation with Marie, I reverted back to my usual prosaic self. With nothing better to do, I browsed through my writings I kept in a large unwieldy scrapbook. I found some notes I had used at a Rotary Club luncheon as the prelude to a new football season in Abilene.

In that program I compared various football formations to the realities of life. I began with the Notre Dame shift made famous by Knute Rockne's great backfield, the *Four Horsemen*. I talked about the single and double wing, and the T-formation with all of its variations.

"*Now the Spread and the Shotgun have arrived,*" I included in the notes. "*But I might add the Shotgun was not derived from any weddings by that name. The point I want to make here today is that in life, as in football, there are those participants who will always find a way to screw it up, regardless of the formation they're in.*

"*So they get penalized and have to punt. Or perhaps I should also say, they won't accept the blame for their mistakes. Then they look for someone else to boot in the rear. Thus, like football, life is a kicking game, and we line up in punt formation just waiting to kick somebody's butt.*"

I thought it was a good link, but some of those upper crust Rotarians thought those comparisons were too raunchy for their gathering. As I closed my scrapbook, I wondered what Geraud Collins would have thought about my remarks as a staunch Baptist preacher. I chose to believe he would have laughed, pumped my hand, and called me *good buddy*.

I pushed my chair away from the desk, thankful that I had no obligations on that scummy day. I was glad to be home and had nowhere else to go.

But the phone rang, and to my surprise it was Brig with a note of high urgency in his voice.

"Kandy, this is not simply another invitation for you to come down here. It's a big, burly plea."

"What's up?" I asked casually. "Why this phone call? Is your computer on the fritz?"

"I wish my problem was that simple. But for Christ's sake, get down here. I need your help. You remember Maydell's old motto, don't you? Well, this is a time for us to care and share."

"All right, Brig. I'll drive down this weekend if the weather isn't too gooey. Right now, that's about all I can promise."

"Kandy, that won't do. I want you to fly down here today and be prepared to stay awhile."

"Are you sick?"

"No, it's nothing like that. But *The Beachcomber* has been invaded by two of the most delectable creatures you could ever imagine."

I was beginning to deplore the riddle. "Brig, what on earth are you talking about?"

THE HELPERS

"My two new helpers, that's what I'm talking about, and I can't handle both of them by myself. Now please hop on the first available flight to Corpus. I'll meet you at the airport. Oh, by the way. I think it would be good if you brought Maydell's old piccolo."

With that word of instruction, Brig abruptly hung up. That caused me to worry what his crazy, gap-filled request was all about.

Routed through a Houston changeover, my plane prepared to land at the Corpus Christie airport late that afternoon. When it cruised over the bay, I got a glimpse of the USS Lexington. It appeared to be deserted, devoid of tourists.

I could not dispel the spooky feeling that in coming to Brig's rescue, I was anything but a tourist or some *Winter Texan*. The rescue, whatever it entailed, somehow involved those new delectable *helpers*. When I stepped out of the plane, I felt like I was sliding into some mysterious plot that only Alfred Hitchcock could concoct.

Brig and I met in the airport terminal. We gave several onlookers a chance to gape when we clamped each other with high fives and our cater cousin hugs. Maybe they wondered why two old guys in their early 70s shared such a communal greeting. But this was the first time in years that we had seen each other. What we immediately noticed were the physical changes in both of us---the retreating gray hair, the eyeglasses, and the pudginess around our middles. Those changes made no difference to us. Brigdon Chouliff and Homan Kandall were together again, even if the purpose remained unclear to me. But whatever the purpose, I knew these two old Baylor classmates would somehow prevail. We were coming directly into each other's life again, and that was our trump card.

I retrieved my large suitcase at the luggage merry-go-round in the terminal. I showed Brig the piccolo case when I grabbed it off the revolving pick-up platform.

"Why this," I asked.

"Oh, let's just say it's a hunch. I've got one of those gut feelings that it could play a major role in the lives of my helpers."

Brig remained hesitant to furnish any other information as we drove to *The Beachcomber*.

When I pressed him for details, what he said only stoked my curiosity.

"Kandy, when we get to my home, you're going to see and hear the damnedest story you have ever heard in your whole life. All I'm going to tell you now is this. Hold on to your breath when you meet those ravishing helpers. Then you'll know why I had to send for you."

The suspense finally ended in Brig's brightly furnished den. He motioned me into a sea-green easy chair that enabled me to behold part of the Corpus Christi Bay. During that gaze I did not realize Brig and I were not alone in the room. When I looked around, I suddenly saw a young Hispanic woman, statuesque in appearance. She stood inside the room by the door.

She moved with panther-like grace toward me. "I am Tondelayo," she said in a canorous voice.

Her words had the same sultry flair that Hedy Lamarr had used for her entrance in *White Cargo*. I could not believe what

THE HELPERS

I saw---a remake of what some people called *the most beautiful woman in the world*. She hovered on one side of my chair.

I looked at Brig in bewilderment. He smiled at my baffled expression.

"You think you're seeing a reincarnation of Hedy Lamarr, don't you? But just wait until you see her sister."

Brig whopped his hands together in a single loud clap.

The signal brought the sister into the den. She likewise was tall and willowy. Her long dark hair tumbled down her shoulders. Like her twin, she was dressed in a white blouse, blue jeans, and sandals. The radiant gleam of her eyes penetrated mine.

"I am Tondelayo," she said in a fierce whisper.

Quietly with the same animal grace of her sister, she moved to the other side of my chair.

I tried to ignore the staged performance. "Where did you find them?" I stammered at last, hoping I had found the right words for this devastating encounter that Brig obviously had planned for its maximum impact.

"Mr. Chonliff didn't find us," said the first Tondelayo. "We found him."

"He is now our *padron*," said the second Tondelayo.

Brig knew that I needed more answers. "Kandy, I promise you will hear the entire story after the dinner these ladies prepare. Right now, just get ready for the best tasting Mexican food that has ever given your stomach the jollies."

"They look like Hedy, they walk like Hedy, they speak like Hedy, and they also cook?"

"We have several specialties," said the second Tondelayo as she took my hand and helped me out of the easy chair.

WILLIAM HORICK

    I had come to *The Beachcomber* thinking I would have to rescue Brig. But now I could plainly see that this would be no easy rescue act. Who, after all, would ever want to be rescued from the heavenly presence of these two beautiful women who impersonated Hedy Lamarr with such guile. I did not bother to ask what their several specialties might be. I already had too many other questions that needed answers.

Chapter Fourteen
The Conquistadors

AS WE DINED on enchiladas and plump, puffy tacos the Tondelayo twins had prepared with much loving care, Brig furnished amazing facts about the young women. They periodically punctuated his remarks with some lurid exclamation points when they lapsed into Spanish.

The twins actually had real life names. They were Carmen and Carmela Monteza. I was convinced Brig could not tell them apart. I didn't even try.

"It all began a couple of weeks ago," said Brig. "After I finished breakfast, I strolled out to the veranda. After I looked across the bay, I suddenly noticed that the cabana had been broken into. When I went down to investigate, I found two clumps of miserable looking humanity on the floor. They had nothing on but tattered scraps of clothing. Then I realized they were twins. One shuddered in the corner in a semi stupor, freaked out that I was there to harm her. The other clump, her frazzled sister, sat beside her. She was barely awake, but she also feared my presence."

"That was me," said the first twin. "I am Carmen Monteza."

"The sight of them startled me," Brig continued. "This was no scavenger hunt boondoggle. I knew they were in some kind of nasty trouble. I asked Carmen what they were doing in the cabana."

Carmen spoke again. "With a deep gasp, I said we're hiding. Some Mexicans are after us."

"Then I said, but you're a Mexican, aren't you?"

Brig smiled at Carmen as he spoke. "She roused herself, still shivering with fright. 'No mister, I am an American, and I speak good English. A drug cartel lobo has been chasing my sister and me. He is a very vile and evil man.'"

I was already awed by the fragmentary story. I glanced at Carmen and Carmela. Their nods agreed with what Brig was saying.

He continued to expand the story. "Are you all right", I asked her. "You both look thoroughly battered."

Carmen confirmed his assessment. "That's right, we are," I told him. "Carmela and I broke into the cabana and spent the night in there. We were exhausted. We had nowhere else to go. We've been on the run ever since we escaped from the cartel in *Nuevo Laredo*. Those *bastardos* held us as captives for three years before we managed to escape."

"We escaped by putting rat poison in our guards' burritos," Carmela smiled. "Those pricks got sick, and we jiggled our little butts out of there in one big hurry." She looked hopefully at me as a penitent child. "Pardon me, Senor Kandy. I didn't mean to say that. I'm sorry."

"That's okay. I've heard a lot of words that are much worse," I said.

THE HELPERS

"The girls had stayed alive by cooking for their captors," said Brig. "I pulled Carmen up and together we brought Carmela up to the house. I found robes for both of them and fixed them something to eat which they gobbled up. I asked how they came to be in *Nuevo Laredo*. Carmen told me that she and Carmela had worked undercover for a Mexican newspaper over there. They hoped to avenge the murder of their parents who were killed in *Nuevo Laredo*. But some stooge on the paper snitched on them to the cartel kingpin, a guy named Mirandez. That's when his thugs abducted them."

Carmela began tidying up the supper table. She scooped up my plate when she spoke again.

"Our parents had been caught in the crossfire of a gunfight between two rival drug gangs on a street in *Nuevo Laredo*," she said. "Mirandez was the leader of one of those gangs. He is scum. When he captured us, he wanted to slash our throats, but we cooked a good meal for him. That's what saved Carmen and me. That pig liked our cooking, and he soon let us take over his kitchen, but that's all the freedom we had."

"Mr. and Mrs. Monteza were American citizens, but they lived and taught school in Mexico," Brig indicated.

"That's true," said Carmen. "Carmela and I were born in Mexico City. But our parents were Americans, and that makes us Americans also, even though we were born in a foreign country. *No es verdad?*"

I spoke for the second time during the intriguing narrative. "Yes, that's right. I know that's the international law."

Brig nodded to the young women. "As I told you, my friend Kandy is a writer. He knows a lot about such things."

He turned toward me as I thanked Carmela for taking my ice tea glass. "*De nada,*" she smiled.

"Kandy, you have only heard dibs and dabs about their ordeal thus far. I haven't told you how they fled across the Rio Grande when the cartel discovered their escape. They got away by hiding in a truck, but they had more problems in Laredo. They went to the Border Patrol station seeking help. The agents there interrogated them hot and heavy about their identity. They couldn't prove their American citizenship because they had no identification papers. So the BP guys assumed they were illegal immigrants. They continued to grill the girls with some unsavory methods."

Carmela returned to the supper table and took over the account of the interrogation.

"One of those dishonorable men told me Carmen and I would be freed if we showed them some special privileges. Mr. Kandy, do you know what I told him? I said, '*Besame cola.*'"

Brig and I had heard enough gutter Spanish to know what the term meant in English. I smiled slyly at Carmela, trying not to embarrass her. This time she did not apologize for her remark.

That didn't matter to me. Considering what I had already heard about Carmen and her, I doubted if profanity ever embarrassed either of them. They probably had learned how to spew out a lot of salty language during their captivity.

Carmen stood and removed Brig's plate. "That's when we both got roughed up," she said. "Lucky for us, some shyster lawyer. . . I think that's the term. . . came along and bailed us out with the promise to the Border guys that he would be responsible for us. But of course he expected us to be his dolls in prostitution. He was taking us to some crummy hotel when we punched him out. He ran his car into a telephone pole. That's when we hopped aboard a eastbound freight train headed toward Brownsville."

Brig resumed his knowledge of the story.

"It was a short ride. They jumped off when the train pulled to a stop in McAllen. That's when they began the most hazardous part of their zigzag escape pattern. They hid in barns and trucks, and even in bus station restrooms. They tried to be as inconspicuous as possible, but being twins they had to resort to trickery. So they tried to disguise themselves any way they could, like how they walked and talked, and looked. Carmen and Carmela also posed as a man and woman one time. They did anything and everything in order to escape both the Border Patrol and Mirandez on their way to Corpus Christi. They were sure their enemies were still after them."

Carmela emphasized that fear. "We also bought blonde wigs and dark glasses with money we made working as barmaids in seedy joints along the river. But we were always afraid the Mirandez *bandidos* or some of those Border Patrol badges would spot us. We always had to be careful. *Muy* careful."

"They existed by bathing in the river and washing their clothes, what little they had, in it," said Brig. "They were always menaced by snakes and insects. Both of them got stung by scorpions. They ate cactus juice at times to stay alive."

"We also raided chicken coops for eggs," added Carmela. "We ate them raw. And we milked a few cows."

"Our best meal was in what Americans call a greasy spoon cafe. That's when we pulled off our brassieres for a bug-eyed customer. In return, he bought each of us a bowl of chili," Carmen said moodily..

"This is absolutely incredible," I sighed. "But why did you both come all the way to Corpus Christi?"

"Coming here was necessary, Carmen told me after I found them collapsed in the cabana," said Brig. "She told me they had to locate an old friend of their parents, a retired judge named Roy Davlin. Mr. Monteza had sent him a copy of family documents showing the girls' date of birth and American citizenship, just in case something happened to him and Mrs. Monteza. Some court records somehow got lost down there, including the twins' birth certificates. So, finding the judge is vital for Carmen and Carmela. Judge Davlin, assuming he's still alive, is probably the only person who can vouch for the girls."

"Judge Davlin probably thinks the cartel killed us", said Carmela. "That is, if he's not dead himself. We only vaguely remember him. He came down to Mexico City a couple of times when we were little girls. We thought he lived here in Corpus, but thus far Mr. Chonliff has been unable to locate him."

Brig finished his iced tea. His face revealed his concern for the failure.

"That's true, I'm sorry to admit. Judge Davlin is not listed in the phone book. The courthouse has no record of him, and the *Caller* shows no obituary for him in its files. Kandy, that's one reason I called you this morning. Carmen and Carmela need help, but I'm stumped going down a one-way street. I've taken care of them since I found them that morning. I bought them some clothes, and I took them to a a clinic where people know me. They asked no questions about my guardianship. The girls were undernourished, but otherwise they got a good health report---no VD or anything like that."

"We're okay now that we've had time to recover from that awful flight down the river," said Carmen.

"But I'm glad you're with us, Kandy. I told the twins all about you. I know they will treasure your friendship."

Carmela glanced at me with the most provocative pair of dark eyes I've ever seen. I embraced those luminous eyes with my own without making any effort to break the hold we suddenly had on each other. Her eyes became enchantingly seductive like Hedy Lamarr's in all of her movies. Carmela Monteza really didn't need Brig to teach her how to pose as *Tondelayo*, I thought.

"Mr. Kandall," she said softly, "I nearly died down there in the cabana. Carmen and I were exhausted physically and emotionally. We had spent the previous night without food on that aircraft carrier in the bay. That was after we sneaked on board with a tour group. Then the next day we came back with another group. Those people glared at us with hate in their eyes all the way back to the dock. We knew the police would come looking for us. That's when we broke into Mr. Chonliff's cabana. It was there that we saw those lights."

"What lights?" I asked.

"Those colored lights outside the house up on the deck, the red light and the green one."

I finally was able to smile. "They're called running lights.

The red light is on the port side, the left side of a ship or a boat. The green light is on the starboard side, the right side. Those running lights are used to show the presence of a ship at night."

Carmela also smiled. "Mr. Chonliff told us you were in the Navy during the war. That's how you know about those lights, isn't it?"

"That's true."

"Those lights were why Carmen and I chose to hide in the cabana. This house showed our favorite colors, and we felt safe at last, especially when Mr. Chonliff found us. Now we're glad you're here. He told us you would also help us."

I do not ordinarily call a young woman I've just met *honey*, but Carmela Monteza was no ordinary young woman, nor was Carmen. They were *conquistadors* who in the late 20th century had endured every kind of hardship while trying to establish their American citizenship. They deserved my admiration and much more.

Brig's seemingly crazy idea of installing those lights now had my full respect. The lights were, in a sense, *The Beachcomber's* version of the Statute of Liberty for the Monteza twins.

"Honey," I told Carmela, "in the morning we'll start a new search for Judge Roy Davlin."

"And Mr. Chonliff has also told us you will tell all about this Hedy Lamarr he had us pretend to be for your pleasure," said Carmen.

"It was a great impersonation. Hedy would marvel at the striking resemblance to her you and Carmela have---the eyes, the voice, everything. Just don't ask me about a certain European movie she made before she came to Hollywood."

Carmela looked at me with a straight, sober face.

"Why, did Hedy do something naughty?"

Brig and I could not control our laughter. It confused the twins initially, but when the laughter did not abate, they smiled at us openly in good will. They had given their old guy protectors a moment of mirth, and that made them radiantly happy. In turn, that pleased Brig and me, knowing that the twins had no happy face during their captivity and escape from the Mirandez cartel.

Chapter Fifteen
Bumper Cars

LATER THAT EVENING, Brig and I sat on the deck upstairs while we sipped Mogen David. It was a starburst night that helped give sparkle to the lights of the cities across the bay. I could also see the outline of the long bridge that connected Corpus Christi to those Coastal Bend towns. The entire area seemed to be one sprawling suburb without any boundaries.

"You've got a great view up here," I remarked.

"Kandy, why don't you move down here and live with me", Brig asked with unexpected candor. "We have a couple of great views downstairs we can share, you know. I'm serious. Why don't you make the move?"

"For a lot of reasons, that's why. I've got strong ties in Waco, for one thing."

Brig placed his wine glass on a small, circular table and looked at me with stark, painful disbelief.

"You've got nothing in Waco except a lot of memories of your Baylor days with Maydell, and your friendship with Hex Grantham. That makes you a harlequin, my friend. You're a

THE HELPERS

clown living in the past. You don't have a sad, painted face like a clown, but I know the pretense you make. It shows. I know because I'm a brother harlequin."

Silently I stood up and walked over to the banister, still impressed with all those lights across the bay on the shoreline. I swallowed the last of my Mogen David,

Brig followed me to the banister and stood at my side.

"Yes, that's a lovely view. But don't you see something else? You and I have been stuck in neutral ever since Freddie and Maydell died. We're like a couple of bumper cars in an amusement park. We've been going around in circles all these years. We bump, and we get bumped. And in the process, we think that's the sum total of life. We need to get out of those stupid bumper cars and go ride the roller-coaster."

"All by ourselves, a couple of old quacks in their early seventies?"

"Not at all. We'll take Carmen and Carmela with us."

"They've already had their roller-coaster ride, haven't they? And besides, we're probably fifty years older than those twin Tondelayos. How old are they?"

Brig chuckled in my ear as he refilled his glass and took a healthy swig.

"Carmen and Carmela are twenty-seven. So the fifty years you guessed is not correct, nor important. The only important thing is all those years of our maturity in their favor. Geez, Kandy. You surely saw how Carmela kept admiring you at the dinner table. She wasn't seeing some old sugar daddy. Carmela sensed a lasting contentment you two could share together. Trust me, Carmela and Carmen aren't interested in some fly-by-night affair, and they're not gold diggers."

"Brig, what the hell is in that Mogen David? You may be on the verge of suggesting that we marry those Hedy twins."

He poured me another glass of the wine with a salutation. "Well, in due time, why not? Crazier things than that happen all the time in this goofy, leapfrog world."

"And I suppose you will also say that Carmen and Carmela should become the mothers of our children," I answered. "But blast it, Brig. You've got to be realistic. We might not have any juice left to get them pregnant."

"True enough," he sighed. "But we could sure have a lot of fun trying."

I hastily downed that second glass of Mogen David.

"Know something, Brig? That's what I like most about your sense of humor. It's always so devilishly subtle."

We were still laughing when we came down to the den. Carmen and Carmela sat on the long sofa, looking quite comfortable and serene after they had washed the dinner dishes and cleaned up the kitchen. But which of the two was Carmela? I could only guess, and I had never liked guessing games.

The twins were not watching TV, but that did not surprise me. I was sure they wanted none of its violence or sordid misdeeds after their perilous adventure down the Rio Grande and along the dangerous corridor of the Texas coast. Those running lights had been a beacon to them, and now they were escapees no longer. Now the Monteza sisters had found a haven in their borrowed home, hopefully safe from their former captors.

THE HELPERS

Brig and I were pleased to see them on the sofa. They were young and lovely, ripe for a new life through masculine gentility and care. They were also Hispanic, a fact that once had aroused my prejudice against such people, especially illegal immigrants like Alonzo Perida and the uncontrollable drug traffic they curried in the southwestern tier of the United States.

But now, as Brig and I stood beside them, I was deeply thankful that the twins had actually fought the cartel. Their gumption convinced me they were attempting to be good patriotic Americans who had risked their lives to uphold the citizenship they were trying to prove. That thought, surely aided by the Mogen David, persuaded me that Carmela and Carmen deserved all the help Brig and I could offer. If that help turned to love, who were we to quarrel with the human heart, or even our memory of Maydell and Freddie Foster?

There was one minor problem that still existed, however. I could see that Brig was still unable to tell the twins apart when they were together.

"How does my friend Brigdon deal with that?" I asked them.

"Is that really important?" Brig laughed.

"It certainly should be," said Carmela. She eyed Carmen with a questioning look. "Why don't we go ahead and show them the way? They don't look like cat and mouse players to me. And Mr. Kandy looks drowsy. He's had a very long day, and perhaps too much wine."

Definitely too much wine, I thought as I gazed serenely at Carmela.

"All right," Carmen agreed. "In the morning at breakfast,

your Tondelayos will reveal how we are different. Then you should be able to recognize us. That would be good, I think."

I slept well that night in one of Brig's three bedrooms, Like all of the house, it had the aura of the sea. A large painting of two bare-breasted mermaids hung over the bed. I blew them a kiss before I retired.

When I awoke the next morning, I had no interest in the mermaids. My only concern was finding Judge Davlin for the Monteza twins. I shaved with my electric razor and slipped into casual gray slacks and a green pullover shirt. Then I climbed the steps up to the terrace deck.

The view from the banister where I had stood last night was breath-taking. The early morning sun slanted its rays on the towns across the bay, Portland and Rockport, Brig had once mentioned. The long bridge over to them was heavy with traffic. As I watched the procession, I sniffed the cool Gulf breeze wafting in from the south. It would be a good day to search for Judge Davlin, perhaps across the bay. The twins had thought he lived in Corpus. I believed his residence might instead be somewhere in the Corpus area, perhaps Portland or Rockport. They at least offered us a starting point in our quest.

I suddenly heard footsteps behind me on the terrace. Spinning around, I spied one of the twins. She wore white shorts and a light gold blouse. Her legs were long and graceful, delightful to behold. She carried a tray that was brimming with food.

"Which Tondelayo are you?" I gulped.

"I am Carmela, and I have brought your breakfast up to you."

"You didn't have to do that."

"No, I didn't, Senor Kandy. But I could hardly serve you breakfast in bed, could I? That would have been improper, don't you think? But out here on this deck with its beautiful view, you can sit back and enjoy my *huevos rancheros*."

"Sit down and have breakfast with me."

"I can't, not this morning at least. Mr. Brigdon always likes to have Carmen and me with him at the breakfast table. It gives him the chance to look at us together while he tries to guess our identity. He says that makes his day."

Those *huevos rancheros* were just part of a breakfast that included half a grapefruit, toast, orange juice, and coffee. Carmela sat with me at the table where Brig and I drank our Mogen David. She smiled, knowing that I enjoyed the meal.

"When are you and Carmen going to show Brig and me how to tell you apart," I asked as I diced the grapefruit. "She said it would be this morning."

"We are wearing our favorite colors this morning. See, I have this ribbon on my shirt. It's green like your shirt. Carmen will have a red ribbon. That will be the difference in how we look. Our colors are like those lights we saw."

"Well, those ribbons will help. But don't you have something more tangible, some mark, perhaps."

"Yes, I do." Carmela leaned over the table, taking my hand in hers. She pushed a cluster of hair from her forehead and ran my fingers across a small scar that I would not have otherwise detected.

"Mirandez scratched me with a piece of broken glass when I dropped a bottle of his tequila. Lucky for me, that cockroach was drunk at the time. I managed to duck away from his full slash."

"I'm thankful you did. That crease on your forehead doesn't mar your beauty, Carmela. Thanks for showing it to me. Now I'll know how to identify you."

"I want you to know all about me, Mr. Kandy."

Her statement reminded me that I had forgotten the diced grapefruit and the cities across the bay. I lowered my hand away from her face. That eliminated the touch, but not the quaint feeling that stirred me inwardly.

"Does Brigdon know about your scar?"

"Carmen will tell him at the breakfast table. He's a late sleeper. My scar won't matter to Mr. Brigdon. He saw a lot of flesh when he found us. He said later that in the future, he would concentrate on navel oranges. That made us laugh. He's a wonderful man. He bought us clothes and has given us his home. Now Mr. Brigdon wants to do a portrait of Carmen and me."

"That's great. Brig has always had an eye for pretty pictures. He's a professional, you know."

"You're a professional too, Mr. Kandy. I like that."

"I am a joker. That's what you'll discover about me."

Carmela smiled as I took her hand for our walk downstairs. "But you're a writer, Mr. Kandy. I want to hear you when you're serious-minded."

It was a happy breakfast table. With lots of playful banter, we learned we could converse with each other openly in good-natured companionship. I enjoyed that. It was like those pleasantries I exchanged with Marie at *Denny's*. But this wasn't *Denny's* or scrambled eggs with hash browns.

This was *huevos rancheros* with picante sauce. This was *The Beachcomber*, and it was Brigdon Chonliff's home. In it we were, to some miraculous extent, a family circle.

True, our future just then was an unknown factor. How long our bond would continue, we did not know. But it was amazingly clear we would not squash our relationship as though it were some poison-tailed scorpion. The girls had been stung by those little monsters during their flight down the Rio Grande, and Brig and I knew we must protect them against more stings of any kind.

But I still lived in Waco, a fact which severely complicated matters.

Chapter Sixteen
Hello, Clarence Budington Kelland

B RIG LIKED MY IDEA for finding Judge Roy Davlin, although he blamed himself for not conducting a more thorough investigation initially.

After he and the girls had breakfast, he drove us across the long high bridge to Portland. We checked out all possible leads, but our inquiries produced no results. That negative search led us to Rockport, a delightful tourist town with its shops and restaurants there on the bay. Rockport also had a myriad of fishing boats that attracted countless forays of seagulls that kept swooping down in the quest for food. Rockport would have been the perfect locale for one of those Clarence Budington Kelland serials in the old *Saturday Evening Post*, I thought.

After several failures to locate Judge Davlin, we stopped at a drug store where a pharmacist warily gave us some positive but confidential information. The judge came there periodically for prescription refills. The pharmacist confirmed that he had an unlisted phone number as we had suspected. He could furnish no other information other than his

THE HELPERS

thought that the judge lived on a houseboat somewhere outside of town.

That scanty information finally led us to the end of our search. We found the houseboat in a sequestered little settlement a couple of miles from downtown Rockport. It was a small, sub-standard looking residence. Judge Roy Davlin was seated on the stern of his houseboat adjusting a fishing rod when we arrived. The old judge had a wizened round face with a goatee. He looked nothing like a man of the judicial system in his overalls and a blue baseball cap that looked older than the man himself.

Judge Davlin eyed us with a tinge of unrest as we stood on the dock next to his floating home. It was quite apparent that unknown callers were not to his liking.

"You are Judge Davlin, aren't you?" I asked.

He responded with a furtive little nod. He clutched the fishing rod tightly as if it were a weapon against unwanted visitors. He also tugged at his old baseball cap as though he were trying to hide his face.

"It's very urgent that we talk with you, Judge Davlin," I said. "These young women are the Monteza twins, Carmen and Carmela."

The judge meandered over to us, still holding the fishing rod like a switch if it became necessary to fight off his intruders. He squinted at Brig and me briefly, but concentrated his gaze upon the girls. He finally graced them with a placid smile.

"Yes, you could be the little Raggedy Anns who belonged to Eduardo and Andrea Monteza," he said. "I couldn't tell you apart even then. Come aboard and let these tired old eyes have a good look."

"We are those Raggedy Anns," said Carmela as we stepped over to the houseboat deck. "And these gentlemen are our *padrons*, Mr. Chonliff and Mr. Kandall. They helped us find you when we discovered you didn't live in Corpus."

"I moved here a long time ago. Rockport is safer than the double C. It's also safer for me to have an unlisted phone number,"

Even as he spoke, Judge Davlin surrendered any fears he had about us. He threw his fishing rod aside and beckoned to us.

"Let's go below where we can palaver," he said. "Actually, I have long hoped you girls were alive, and would be able to find me. I'm afraid, however, that I have some distressing news for you."

"About our citizenship papers?" asked Carmen.

"No, I have them. They're safe."

Inside his cramped living quarters, the judge told of alarming developments since the twins escaped from *Nuevo Laredo*. Although he was small in stature, he spoke with a strong, stentorian voice.

"The cartel is still hunting you because you know too much about it. I know this to be true because I have sources along the Rio Grande. I also know some things about how you escaped. I figured you would try to locate me. But so did the cartel kingpin, the man known as Mirandez."

When Judge Davlin paused momentarily, Carmela spoke again.

"He and his goons held us captives. Mirandez is garbage."

"Indeed he is," the judge continued. "But he's also resourceful, and he has plenty of *dinero* to get what he wants.

THE HELPERS

And right now, I've heard he has a fanatical desire to kill you both because you poisoned his henchmen. My sources informed me that's the way Mirandez plans to murder you. He almost caught you when you got to Brownsville, but somehow you managed to elude his gang."

"We found some kind of sand operation on the river near Brownsville," said Carmen. "We hid out there and made a little money shoveling sand onto dump trucks. That enabled us to ride a bus up to Kingsville. The driver got us by the Border Patrol checkpoint. Then we made it over to Padre Island. We stayed there on the island all the way to Corpus. We traveled mostly at night after we found scraps of food that campers had left. Luckily, some old fisherman found us and gave us a ride part of the way."

"You *senoritas* have been very brave," Judge Davlin said. "And you are *muy lindisima*. You both look like movie stars. But I must again warn you that you and these gentlemen are in grave danger. I advise you to find a good hiding place and remain holed up. You just need to hope to God that Mirandez doesn't find you. You've eluded him miraculously thus far, but miracles do end, I'm sorry to say."

"What about police protection in Corpus?" asked Brig.

The judge stroked his goatee, as he had done during the conversation.

"The Corpus police and immigration authorities have also been looking for the girls. That tour group from the Lex tattled to the cops, I understand. They believe you are illegal immigrants who stowed away with those tourists."

"But now we can prove our citizenship, can't we?" Carmela asked hopefully.

Whatever hope she held for Carmen and herself was quickly dashed by Judge Davlin.

He eyed her remorsefully. "I've got your papers, But they won't matter to Mirandez. If the police find you, he will hear about it. And if that happens, he'll find some way to get to you. He's one bad *hombre* who has connections on both sides of the Rio Grande. Mirandez thrives on corrupt politicians and dishonest cops on the lookout for easy money."

The judge walked slowly to a wall safe that was hidden behind a large painting of the Virgin Mary. He handed a set of documents to Carmen.

"These are your birth certificates and other Monteza family papers. I have guarded them well at your father's request. Now I suggest that you take them and leave here immediately. You see, I've had judicial cases involving the cartel. Those people know me and they may track me down just as you did. I wish I could invite you to have a big fish fry with me so we could really get acquainted, but your safety is more important."

Judge Davlin wrote Brig's name and phone number on a notepad beside his phone.

"I'll call you when and if I hear anything helpful," he promised. "But be careful about other phone calls you may get. Mirandez has a bag full of tricks at his disposal."

We thanked Judge Davlin for his help. But as we drove away from his solemn little houseboat, I had a gnawing gut feeling that we would never hear from him. The judge had tried to hide his own fear of the cartel, but I saw his apprehension by the nervous habit he had of stroking his goatee continually.

THE HELPERS

Unknown to us, Judge Davlin quickly made a phone call to his friend, Detective Tony Delgado at the Rockport police department. It was a phone call that ultimately would save four lives---ours.

Despite the judge's warning, Brig wanted to celebrate. Against my better judgment, he drove up the highway to a well-known seafood restaurant called *The Big Fisherman*.

"Relax, Kandy," he said when we arrived at the parking lot. "There's always a huge noon crowd here, truckers and drillers, lots of working slobs with hard hats. We won't be noticed, and we do have to eat."

"Oh yeah. Eat, drink, and be merry for tomorrow we die," I quipped. I glanced at the twins who were huddled together on the back seat. "I'm sorry that slipped out. But let's play it as safe as we can. Remove those ribbons, and let's go in separately. We'll eat at different tables, and not leave together. Okay?"

Brig nodded. "Kandy, I'm sorry I got you involved in this puddle of puke."

I tapped him on the shoulder. "You don't have to apologize. In Rockport this morning I was thinking how it would feel to be one of those adventurous characters Clarence Budington Kelland wrote about in *The Saturday Evening Post*."

Brig and Carmen entered *The Big Fisherman* first. Carmela and I allowed them several minutes to be seated in the octagonal shaped dining area. Carmela tightly held onto my arm while we waited for a table.

She showed no trepidation. "Homan, this is like being on a first date, except we don't have a chaperone," she giggled.

"Well sweetheart, I just hope it won't be our last date."

That was another blurt remark, but I wasn't ashamed of it. Carmela was now on a first name basis with me, and that caused twitters on my old heart strings. I was feeling young and giddy again, and to hell with Mirandez wherever he was.

The Big Fisherman had a fabulous menu that included every kind of seafood. The menu also included *the catch of the day*. But judging by the way customers stared at us, Carmela was the real catch of the day that some old coot had somehow managed to hook.

Our hostess blinked as she showed us to a table. She had also seated Brig and Carmen at a table across the restaurant from us, and now she gasped, realizing there were *twin* ravishing beauties who demanded attention from everyone, including waiters who carried big oval trays of seafood, one of which got dropped and splattered on the floor.

Carmela and I had crab cakes for an appetizer.

"I wonder what Carmen and your friend Brigdon are having," she mused.

'It's quite apparent they're having a good time. We might as well join them. By now everyone in this place has seen us. Maybe there's safety in numbers."

"I'll give those truckers and hard hats something to think about," Carmela said brazenly, "and it won't be their seafood plates."

I left a small tip for the waiter who served us the crab cakes. With the small plates in hand, Carmela and I strolled across the floor. Well actually, she didn't stroll. Better said, Carmela snaked. Twisting her hips in a wanton display of

THE HELPERS

sensuality, she reminded me of Lauren Bacall in *To Have And Have Not*.

Carmela furnished an explanation for her seductive sway. "A poor frightened, illegal female would never do what I did, would she?"

She eased up to the table where Brig and Carmen sat. Her hip-swaying performance also reminded me of how audacious Maydell could be at times. I had never objected to those stunts Maydell pulled, and now I could only smile at Carmela.

I'll be seeing you in all the old familiar places; that this heart of mine embraces, all day through...

But now I was seeing Carmela Monteza, and she had all the same physical lure that Maydell always possessed in our private moments of sexual pleasure. I was ready to sit down and eat, thinking that would chase away the vibes that came upon me when Carmela began her alluring floorshow.

Our shrimp platters there at *The Big Fisherman* were delicious beyond description. For an added delight, Brig and I dipped hush puppies into a savory New Orleans tartar sauce and fed them to the twins.

But they were the last thing the four of us would enjoy that day.

Carmen suddenly unleashed a fearful shriek.

"It's him. I saw Mirandez," she cried. "He ducked out of sight, but I saw him, and he made sure I did. That *iguana* knows we're here."

We scurried out of *The Big Fisherman*, not waiting for our change from the cashier.

On the parking lot we discovered that all four tires on

Brig's station wagon were flat. It was quite obvious that it had been sabotaged deliberately while we dined. It was no simple act of vandalism by some juvenile hooligan. It had to be a warning from Mirandez who somehow had tracked us to the popular restaurant.

I suddenly remembered what Judge Davlin had said about poison. I did not want to think that our food in *The Big Fisherman* had been laced with some slow-acting poison. I vainly tried to shake off the thought, but I could not. I simply had to ponder it alone.

We quickly herded the girls back inside the restaurant. Now trembling with fear, they knew what Mirandez was capable of doing, anytime, anywhere. I tried to calm them while Brig phoned for roadside assistance his automobile insurance provided.

It was over three hours before we returned to *The Beachcomber*. Brig's telephones began ringing even before we could decide what options we had. Brig nervously lifted the nearest receiver, but in one brief moment he stood spellbound. He motioned for me to come and hear the decidedly Mexican accent of the caller.

"We're very sorry about those flat tires, *gringo*, but that gave us time to come to your house and leave, what's the Yankee term. . .our calling card."

"Where are you?" Brig demanded.

"You don't need to know that, *amigo*."

"All right, Mirandez. I know who you are. What the devil do you want?"

"Your cooperation, *hombre*. Send one of the twins to the phone. It doesn't matter which one. Just do it *muy pronto*."

Brig slammed down the receiver without another word. But instantly the phone rang again. He handed me the receiver and raced to the kitchen phone.

We heard Mirandez speak again. "That was *muy stupido, gringo*. Now send Carmen or Carmela to your phone if you value your home and your place of business. Like I said, we have left our calling card. Mebbe you'll find it in time, but then mebbe you won't. *Que sera sera.*"

Brig motioned for me to send Carmen to the phone. She was breathing heavily when she picked it up.

"Yes?" she whispered.

"I must congratulate you and your sister for your escape," said Mirandez in an oily voiced overture. "I'm glad you spotted me at that restaurant. I planned it that way. I wanted you to know that I'm around, and that you won't escape again. You cunning little foxes have caused me a lot of problems, you know. Now I want to see you both down at the beach. Then we'll go for a nice little boat ride. Just come out of that house this minute. Otherwise, you will face a messy murder investigation."

"Mirandez, you slimy *diablo*, we poisoned your lobos in self defense. They boasted they were going to rape us."

Mirandez laughed coarsely. "I'm talking about the murder of your *compadre*, Judge Davlin. You and your *gringo* friends were seen at his houseboat today shortly before his death. That makes you the prime suspects. *Comprende?*"

Carmen could say nothing in return. She handed me the phone and crumpled to the floor.

"You don't have to speak," said Mirandez impatiently. "But I'm warning you, get out of that house, both of you, and walk slowly down to the beach."

"We're calling the police, you crazy bastard," I snapped. Mirandez hung up before I could say anything else.

Brig returned from the kitchen phone. Seeing Carmen clumped on the floor, he knelt down beside her.

"Kandy, call the police. I'll give you the number."

The phone rang again, and I took the call. Some cop told us not to worry. He said the Corpus police were after Mirandez and had been able to trace his calls to *The Beachcomber*. He advised us to wait there for the arrival of two officers the department was sending to aid us.

Brig assisted Carmen to the long couch where she sank into Carmela's lap.

The fading afternoon sun began casting shadows in *The Beachcomber*. My wristwatch indicated it was nearly five o'clock. None of us said anything. We were trance-like in our glances at each other. We could only hope the police would arrive quickly and protect us from Mirandez.

I knew it was up to them. Our dilemma was beyond any help that Clarence Budington Kelland could ever hope to script in *The Saturday Evening Post*.

Chapter Seventeen
Protective Custody

DETECTIVE SGT. BORRIS MACLARD stood at the front door a few minutes later. He quickly flashed his ID as he introduced himself. He was broad-faced with hefty shoulders. With him was a muscular black policewoman who had the size to mash an entire Roller Derby team off the track with one heavy block. She identified herself as Officer Sharonda Willis, but I wondered if she perhaps didn't moonlight as a wrestling behemoth.

They had been assigned by the Corpus police department to secure our protection, we were told. Both of them were plainclothes cops.

Brig ushered them into the den. "We're certainly glad to see you. We've been threatened this afternoon by a Mexican drug lord."

"Yes, we know about that", Maclard said. He then asked us to identify ourselves. He said nothing substantial as Brig and I spoke. He kept eyeing the twins.

"All right, Mr. Chonliff, we know you are a local businessman. You own a photography studio. So how did you get mixed up with these escapees? We heard the cartel has been looking for them."

"They were fleeing from the kingpin, a guy named Mirandez," I said.

"Yes, we also know about him," Maclard responded. "And you, Mr. Kandall, why are you here?"

He had a voice that sounded contemptible like actor Dan Seymour had in his Nazi role in *To Have And Have Not*.

"I came at my friend's request."

"What was the nature of your request, Mr. Chonliff?"

Brig answered grumpily. "It was a personal matter. "Look, Sergeant Maclard. You're wasting time with these petty questions. Mirandez called and threatened all of us. He implied that a bomb or something lethal is hidden in this house. We also think he may have killed Judge Roy Davlin, a friend of these young women."

Maclard eased up. "Mr. Chonliff, I'm sorry I came on so hard. But we're close to nailing Mirandez. I didn't want to mention Judge Davlin's murder. We didn't want to frighten any of you unduly. That's also why Officer Willis and I came here in an unmarked car, and not a police cruiser. We can't take any chances with your welfare. We know how dangerous and unscrupulous Mirandez can be. The fact is, Officer Willis and I have instructions to hold all of you here in protective custody. So please bear with us. Your safety is our primary concern."

"What about the possible bomb?" I asked. "When Mirandez called, he admitted that he delayed us at *The Big Fisherman* to give him time to come here and plant, what he said, was his calling card."

THE HELPERS

Officer Willis spoke for the first time.

"Did you find anything suspicious?"

"Hell no," Brig replied. "We've had no opportunity to make any search."

Maclard offered a modicum of assurance, raising his hands.

"Sir, we know how Mirandez operates. Planting bombs is not his m.o. That's not his style at all. However, as a precaution, Officer Willis will go through you home and check for anything that looks suspicious."

He nodded to the policewoman to begin the search. To us he said, "I'm sure Mirandez was bluffing about hiding any explosives. He was just trying to scare the dog crap out of you."

"Well, he succeeded," Brig grumbled.

The massive Sharonda Willis was gone for several minutes. When she returned, she carried both of the piccolo cases.

"What's in these?" she asked.

"Piccolos," said Brig. "Those musical instruments belonged to two women, my fiancée and Mr. Kandall's wife. We've had them for many years as keepsakes."

"Open them," Maclard ordered.

Officer Willis complied. She held the piccolos momentarily while she examined them. By her nonchalant way of handling them, it was clear Willis knew nothing about piccolos as musical instruments or potential weapons. She dismissed them rather flippantly. Both Brig and I noticed her flawed inspection.

Carmen and Carmela were fascinated by the piccolos.

Carmela asked for one of them. Maclard gave his approval after making his own clumsy inspection.

Willis handed Maydell's piccolo to Carmela.

Carmela put it to her lips and produced a couple of harsh sounding tweets.

I laughed because I was sure Maydell had made a similar raucous sound the first time she tried to play a piccolo.

Maclard cringed at the noise Carmela created, but he managed to smile.

"Look, we don't need any piccolo lessons," he said. "We're going to be together here for awhile. So I'm going to call out for hamburgers and fries for all of us. Okay?"

No one objected to the consideration. It appealed to us because at the time we needed a good will gesture from the Corpus Christi police department to relieve our mounting tension.

The sergeant picked up the phone and dialed a number with his back turned toward us.

"The works?", he asked when he faced us after he dialed.

We nodded our agreement, and Maclard placed the order for six hamburgers with everything on them, along with the French fries.

"Headquarters will pick up the tab," he said. "Now I suggest that we all just sit back and relax while we wait for the delivery."

"I have to go take a leak," I said. "Okay?"

"Did you search the bathrooms, Willis?"

"No problems, Sergeant," she answered.

I tried not to scramble down the hall to the nearest bathroom, but it was expedient that I relieve myself. Yet as I stood at the commode, I could not relieve myself of a hideous thought.

THE HELPERS

My instincts kept warning me that something about the protective custody order stunk like limburger cheese and chitterlings all mixed together in a smelly pot of bilge that would have gagged even the Macbeth witches Hex Grantham had once mentioned. For one thing, the inspection of *The Beachcomber* by Officer Willis seemed much too easy and quick. And how well trained for the search was she? The Corpus police department surely had a skilled bomb squad that would look in all the right places for all the wrong things.

As for MacLard, why did he make sure that none of us saw the phone number he dialed? His whole demeanor appeared to be a well-rehearsed performance. I had watched a lot of movie actors in my life, and I knew how they staged their role. This guy Maclard could well be following a script like Thomas Gomez, one of my favorite supporting actors, I thought. I also wondered if Mirandez had possibly tapped Brig's phone. Maybe that was the calling card he had mentioned. Or could it be some kind of poison?

I flushed the commode, but I could not flush away my suspicions. When I returned to the den, MacLard was again examining one of the piccolos.

"You know," he said glibly, "these piccolos are quite interesting little music tooters. They look like they could be hollowed out to smuggle drugs."

I asked a sarcastic question. "Or why not blow guns to shoot poison darts like in some jungle movie, Sergeant?"

"That's an interesting idea, Mr. Kandall. It shows that we may never truly appreciate the full extent of the criminal mind," he smiled.

Chapter Eighteen
Burgers and Old Lace

DETECTIVE TONY DELGADO of the Rockport Police Department tried to return Judge Roy Davlin's phone call that afternoon when he learned we had been victimized at *The Big Fisherman*. When the judge did not answer, Delgado sped to the houseboat fearing the worst.

Inside the dwelling he found Judge Davlin's body sprawled on the floor, fatally stabbed. The crime plunged Delgado into a hellhole of despair as he viewed his dead friend. Strong and wiry, a former star athlete at Rockport High School, Delgado vowed to himself that he would find the judge's killer. He quickly suspected Mirandez. Judge Davlin had informed him about meeting the Monteza twins who had eluded the drug baron. Since they had found the Davlin houseboat, Tony Delgado reasoned that Mirandez had found it also and then followed the women to *The Big Fisherman*.

Delgado learned from Davlin's neighbors that a car had pulled to a halt a short distance from the houseboat. The occupants waited until two elderly men in company with two beautiful young women left the houseboat, waving to the judge. After their station wagon moved away, the other car followed them. Then later that car returned and two men entered the houseboat. One of them, according to the neighbors, fit the known description of Mirandez. That wasn't proof, but it was a lead Delgado needed.

When Tony Delgado probed the murder scene, he found a notepad lodged in Judge Davlin's hand. It revealed, in small, delicate handwriting, the name and address of Brigdon Chonliff, along with his Corpus phone number. That concerned Delgado because he knew Brig, having had a family portrait made at his photography studio a few weeks earlier.

The note also included something else the judge had evidently scribbled before he died. Those two words were hardly legible. They made no sense to Tony Delgado when he saw them---*poisoned hamburgers.*

Those words puzzled the young detective who thankfully was in real life, much more than the comic strip character *Dick Tracy* or the fictional *Sherlock Holmes.* Tony Delgado was totally dedicated to his work in law enforcement, and with Judge Davlin's murder, that dedication spurred him into a driving passion to find Mirandez. He also believed that Brigdon Chonliff held the key to the words *poisoned hamburgers.*

Tony Delgado promptly touched base with the Corpus police department. It was there that a police captain told him they believed Mirandez was somewhere in the city, but they didn't know anything about Brigdon Chonliff or the whereabouts of the twin women who had fled from the *Lexington* tour group. The department wasn't sending out bloodhounds in search of them, the captain informed Delgado.

"Mirandez is the prize. We're looking for him, not those women," he said.

"Then you haven't assigned anyone to interview Mr. Chonliff?"

"Not yet at least, but if he holds a connection to the Davlin murder, we'll certainly help you, Lieutenant."

Tony Delgado showed him the crumpled note, and explained his personal interest in apprehending Mirandez.

"Judge Davlin knew the women and my theory is that he was trying to protect them. I know they visited him before Mirandez arrived. Those twins know Mirandez, and he's also out to kill them. Until today at *The Big Fisherman,* they were last seen on the bay beach close to where Brigdon Chonliff lives. They've got to be the reason Mirandez is here in Corpus. He must know they have been staying at Mr. Chonliff's home."

The captain agreed. "Yes, I think you have some interesting pieces of the puzzle. But what's your opinion about the poisoned hamburgers?"

"Sir, I'm not sure. But my guess is Judge Davlin heard Mirandez plotting to kill the twins and their friend Chonliff and the other man with poisoned hamburgers. That's probably why Mirandez stabbed him, but somehow the judge lived long enough to scribble those words before he died. They were a warning to Mr. Chonliff and the people with him."

"You have a very intriguing theory, that's for sure. Lieutenant Delgado, the Davlin murder is in your jurisdiction. I presume you want to follow your idea all the way to the rainbow's end."

Tony Delgado shook the captain's hand. "Sir, you bet your sweet badge I do."

THE HELPERS

"Very well. We'll have people ready to back you up. Just keep us posted on what you find. And good luck. Since you're dealing with Mirandez, you'll need it."

Brig's telephone rang unexpectedly, jolting the twins as it did. Maclard allowed Brig to answer, but he monitored the call on the den phone.

"Hello, Mr. Chonliff," the caller said. "This is Tony Delgado. You recently did a family portrait for me. Remember?"

Brig of course remembered. He also remembered that Tony Delgado was a Rockport cop who wouldn't be calling just then about a family portrait. Brig, like me, had become leery of Maclard. With Maclard on the other phone, Brig made a hasty decision.

"Yes, Mr. Delgado, I remember you. I hope you've been pleased with the portrait. Your twin daughters were absolutely perfect for the sitting."

Tony Delgado paused momentarily, realizing something was amiss because he didn't have twin daughters. "I would like for them to say hello to you."

Maclard signaled Brig to break off the conversation.

"That would be very nice, Mr. Delgado, but right now we have company. We're getting ready to have a hamburger supper."

"That's okay, Mr. Chonliff. I understand. Goodbye."

I knew by how pale he looked after hanging up the phone that Brig had something to tell me, but not in front of Maclard and Willis.

"One of my customers," was all he said.

Sharonda Willis returned to the kitchen to finish setting the table. She once more shunned the twins' offer to help her. That bothered me. For all I knew, Sharonda Willis could be in there dishing out some kind of poison.

The rest of us sat in silence. I offered to turn on the local evening news, but Maclard objected.

"Leave the TV alone," he barked. "There could be news about the Davlin murder that would only give you folks more jitters. Mirandez might learn that we have you in protective custody, and that would complicate things. Please follow my instructions. I need your cooperation."

I stepped away from the TV and sat down. I kept hoping the hamburgers would arrive soon, but I knew that none of us were actually thinking about food, especially Carmen and Carmela. They still sat stiffly on the long couch. The way Maclard kept looking at their bare legs, I sensed the increased apprehension they felt.

"Sergeant, why not let the girls go change clothes," I suggested. "They've got a bad case of the shivers."

"Officer Willis is busy. She doesn't have time to stop and play nursemaid with them. Just relax. The hamburgers should be here any minute now."

"That's absurd, Sergeant," Brig growled. "These ladies aren't babies. They don't need Officer Willis to watch them change clothes."

"Sir, we have to go by the book," he said shakily.

Or perhaps by the script, I thought. It appeared that Maclard was coming unglued as though he lost his script and was having to ad-lib without any Tele Prompter. It also became clear the hamburger delivery was late, a fact that caused Maclard to pace around the room like some caged animal.

He scowled at me when I spoke again.

"Sergeant, your nerves are showing. You should set a better example for all of us."

"Shut up, Kandall. I don't need your crappy advice." He offered no apology for his remark.

I prodded him again. "Who's making those hamburgers, Sergeant? Personally, I like the kind that *Whataburger* cooks up. They're not saturated with grease the way some of those other places do a lube job on their meat. I especially enjoy those *Whataburgers* with cheese. Do you think our burgers will have cheese? And will they have mayo or mustard? Personally, I prefer mustard. I think mayo is better suited for salad than hamburgers. Which will we be getting, Sergeant?"

Carmen and Carmela finally smiled. They were enjoying the hopscotch word game I seemed to be playing with Maclard.

"How should I know" he snapped.

"You ordered them, didn't you? You asked us if we wanted the works."

"Kandall, I told you to shut up."

"I was just trying to make conversation. To relieve the tension, you know." I said nothing else, but I could tell Maclard had become thoroughly unraveled.

He sprang to the front door when someone rang the bell. He opened the door, and to his bewilderment, there stood Tony Delgado posing as the deliveryman with a large hamburger sack in his hand.

Maclard tried to shove the door shut. "You're not our man," he shouted.

"I'm his substitute," said Delgado, pushing inside. "Your guy's now in police custody, and so are you, Maclard. You're under arrest." He pushed Maclard into the den, brandishing his service revolver in his other hand.

"On what charge," Maclard asked.

"How about posing as a cop for a starter. But we'll tack on some other goodies like attempted murder, believe me. Meanwhile, help yourself to one of these hamburgers. You like hamburgers, don't you, Maclard?"

Maclard tried to squirm away. "Sharonda, get in here," he yelled.

Officer Willis bolted in from the kitchen when she heard Maclard's shrill cry. She reached in her purse for a small pistol. When the twins realized her intent, they leaped on both sides of her ample body. Their attack looked like the old football high/low. Her pistol fell to the floor. Willis almost succeeded in shaking Carmen off, but Carmela bit her beefy arm. Willis tried to swing her purse at her, but Carmen reacted by looping her arm around Willis's throat. Carmela finished the bout by pulling her down to the floor when Brig and I joined the fray. Both twins kneed Big Sharonda in the ribs while we pinned her thighs. It wasn't a pretty scene, but Willis lay there, a wounded buffalo silent and subdued.

Tony Delgado nudged her and Maclard with his revolver. He had them spread themselves, face down, on the floor.

"These people are narcs," he explained to us. "We know all about them. They're part-time actors who stooge for Mirandez. In return for the dirty work they do for him, he

THE HELPERS

keeps them supplied up with drugs. They were going to kill all of you with poisoned hamburgers."

Uniformed police officers rushed in and handcuffed Maclard and Sharonda Willis before herding them outside to Corpus Christi patrol cars.

She snarled at Maclard. "Damn it Borris, this is a helluva way to spend what could have been our wedding night."

"Tony, where is Mirandez" asked Brig.

"The Corpus police have him in custody for the murder of Judge Davlin. They nailed him when he drove up a few minutes ago. He wanted to be here when all of you died slowly from the poison he planted in your hamburgers. It was going to be his fiendish act of revenge for what happened in *Nuevo Laredo*."

Tony Delgado stood by with a broad, toothy smile. He shook hands with the twins.

"Young ladies, that was quite a whammy you put on Sharonda Willis. She's a tough, bitchy hellcat, but you knocked her on her can. Thanks."

"*De nada*," said Carmen. "Carmela and I are proud of our American citizenship. We just wanted to help."

"Well, all of you can now relax," said Delgado, still beaming. "Enjoy the evening. We'll keep the media people away from you for awhile. Oh, by the way. The burgers I brought in are safe to eat, unless of course you prefer something else. We'll use the poisoned ones as evidence. The Corpus police also caught the guy who was going to deliver them for Mirandez. He was with Mirandez at Judge Davlin's houseboat."

"We had planned to watch an old movie tonight," I said. "*Arsenic and Old Lace.*"

"It sounds interesting," said Delgado. "What's it about?"

"Lieutenant, it's a dark comedy about two warped elderly sisters," I indicated. " They poison lonely old gentlemen with their elderberry wine when they come to their house looking for room and board. But now I think we'll skip that movie. We'll just enjoy your hamburgers for our supper. But without any elderberry wine, of course."

He laughed as Brig walked with him to the front door.

"Tony, thanks for saving us. I made a mistake. I should have called you when I found the twins. That could have prevented all this. But I'm thankful that you caught my signal that something was wrong when I mentioned your twin daughters. I remembered quite well that you don't have twin daughters."

"Yes sir, I guessed that, and when you mentioned hamburgers, I knew for sure you were in trouble."

"Well, to show my gratitude for how you saved us, I want to do another family portrait for you, free of charge."

"Sir, that would be nice, but I thought you had retired."

Brig patted him on the back. "I'm changing that stance. Now I've got a family responsibility. I want to involve these young women in what's left of my life."

Tony Delgado paused at the door. "Take good care of them. They will surely be called to testify against Mirandez. They can also bust his drug cartel in *Nuevo Laredo* wide open if they are willing to take the risk."

Carmela spoke with no hesitation.

"Officer, we know all about risks, and we're willing to take more of them if we can somehow help to get rid of that scumball Mirandez. We learned a lot about him and

THE HELPERS

his business while Carmen and I were his captives. How do you say it? Blow the whistle? That's what we'll do. My sister and I are very proud to be Americans and to do something helpful."

She waved her arms in salutation to Brig and me. "And we want these gentlemen to be proud of us as if we were their daughters."

I broke the silence Carmela's words had pinned upon us after Tony Delgado left.

"Brig, your friend Tony is quite a detective. He's even better than old Charlie Chan."

"Who is Charlie Chan," asked Carmen.

"He was a Chinese detective character in a lot of old movies back in the late '30s and early '40s. He was always popping up in different places. Charlie was fond of saying, 'Thank you so much.'"

Carmela bowed to me. "Homan, that's what Carmen and I want to say to you and Brigdon. Thank you so much."

Chapter Nineteen
Reality on the Half Shell

BRIGDON AND I danced with our *daughters* that night to celebrate their liberation. We swayed around the floor on that entrancing evening as though we had no intention of letting tomorrow intrude.

The music came from an old cassette Brig had kept. It brought the well-suited big band sound to us as we twirled the twins around the den. The girls were surprisingly graceful, much more than Brig and me. In the war, Brig had loved to jitterbug with bobby sox partners, jostling them around on a lot of dance floors that catered to military personnel. With Maydell, I had been no Fred Astaire, but we loved the slow tempo of a waltz.

I wanted to waltz with Carmela, but Brig and I compromised by gently two-stepping with her and Carmen. The four of us danced fluidly around the room at arms' length, at least initially. But as the evening wore on, Brig and I deftly held the Monteza sisters close to us. We no longer saw them as our *daughters*.

They made no attempt to pull away from our embraces,

even when our right hands rested on the small of their backs. Perhaps the flow of Mogen David after our hamburger supper made us that bold. I chose, however, to believe that the wine had nothing to do with Carmela resting her head on my shoulder as we continued to dance. And I could see that Carmen followed her lead as she nestled up to Brig.

The Beachcomber suddenly became a melodic dreamland. I knew that the old coots had something to say in private to their dance partners. I led Carmela out to the veranda. We stood there holding hands as we exchanged glances that were silent soliloquies about our feelings.

Neither of us cared to speak. The dialogue between our hearts needed no oral elaboration.

Carmela kissed me gently on the cheek.

I retaliated by lightly pressing my lips against hers. She then pinned her arms around my neck, and her next kiss was long and blissful. I finally broke her embrace, but I could not escape the fragrance of her dark, delirious eyes.

"This can't be real," I said softly.

"But Homan, it is real. You and I both know it is. I'm not Tondelayo. . .some character in a movie, whoever she was."

"No Carmela, you're not Tondelayo. She was not a nice person. I would prefer to call you Dulcinea. But neither am I Don Quixote who chased windmills with his impossible dream. I am merely a lonely old man. I was married, but I've been a widower for many years. I deeply loved my wife, so much that I never wanted to fall in love again. But now something has happened between you and me that I can't quite describe, not even as a writer."

"You don't have to describe love, to yourself or to me.

I will give you love, every last ounce that's possible to give. That's all you need to know," she whispered.

"You're forgetting that there's too much disparity in our ages, Carmela."

She kissed me again. "Carmen and I speak good English, but we do not know some of the words. What is disparity?"

"It means a difference. You need to understand that I'm too old for you, just like Brig is too old for Carmen. All of us have to be realistic."

"We had to be realistic this afternoon before the police rescued us. Now, we don't because being realistic overlooks how you and I feel about each other. That mutual feeling is something we cannot ignore."

I turned away, choosing not to face her. "Our vast age difference is what we cannot ignore."

"Unless people are cowards, they can," she answered.

Carmela stepped around in front of me to counter my move. She faced me with severity in her eyes.

"There, that's much better. Now I'm face to face with you again. And I'm not looking at the face of a coward. I'm seeing a just and honorable man who has some needs that I can satisfy as his helper. Homan, you don't need some clucking old hen for that. You need me. Look, let's face facts. If you're really going to be realistic, you can tell we need each other. That is, unless you think my Hispanic brown skin is not suitable for your Anglo good taste."

"No Carmela, that's not true. That might have been true years ago after my wife was killed by a Mexican soused with dope, but now it's not. I see you only as a beautiful young woman. You're fresh and appealing, and that's exactly the problem. I'm stale and withered. That makes it hard for me to even live with myself, much less anyone like you. I cannot offer you that kind of pilfered life, and I won't. I want you to understand that. Please try."

This time Carmela did not respond. She turned away and walked sullenly back into the den. There Brig and Carmen were still twirling around on their makeshift dance floor. They paid no attention to Carmela or me when I followed her to the dancers.

Any mixed emotions Brig had about Carmen were certainly not evident. He spun her around in an underarm spree and leaned over her as he bent her backward. It was a great display of an oft-used dance routine that would have been an eye-popper on any ballroom floor. Carmen was obviously enjoying the jitterbug whirl Brig had foisted upon her.

I smiled at them before glancing at Carmela. She made no attempt to look at me. She brushed past the dancers and sped away to her room.

Carmen and Brig finally stopped dancing when they realized Carmela was emotionally wounded, but the big band sound lingered, loud and raucous. In her haste to leave, I saw Carmela dab a teardrop from her eye.

At the breakfast table the next morning I announced that I needed to fly back to Waco that day. My reasons were hardly impeccable. I told Brig and the twins that I had business and personal matters to transact. It wasn't a bare-faced lie, but neither was it an example of shining truth.

Carmela jabbed at her grapefruit, but said nothing. I glanced at Carmen, and she also remained wordless. I had to assume that by the eerie silent treatment heaped upon me,

Carmela had informed Brig and her sister about the abrupt end to our conversation on the veranda.

Brig got me booked on my return flight that afternoon. He drove me to the airport, saying little. But in the terminal before I boarded my plane, he unloaded his scathing firepower on me. Old Brigdon Chonliff was a waist gunner again, and he was determined to shoot me down.

"Kandy, you're running away. You damn well know that, don't you? There's no reason for your all-fired hurry to get back to Waco. It's just an excuse to escape from Carmela."

"I have to escape. She practically proposed to me last night. I'm not ready for that kind of power play."

"Bull taco. How ready do you have to be? Six months? A year? You've already waited much too long after Maydell's death. You keep playing your stupid waiting game and all the sugar cookies will be gobbled up. There won't be any left in the jar."

"What about you and Carmen?"

Brig continued his scathing assault. "Man alive, Kandy. Don't you know your old buddy Brigdon is a speed demon? I proposed to her last night during your crash dive on the veranda. That was the reason for the fling we were having when you came in. Carmen and I were thinking about a double wedding sometime this summer. But now it looks like you've fouled up that nectar. Now blast it, just go catch your plane and enjoy your flight, even though you're empty-headed and empty-handed."

Minutes later I was in the air over the Corpus Christi Bay. Again I briefly spotted the USS Lexington. Only now it was the Yorktown in its duel to the death with those

Japanese warplanes at Midway. Even worse, I then saw myself jumping overboard to escape an oncoming dive bomber named Carmela Monteza.

A flight attendant asked me if I desired something to drink. Ordinarily I would have said no to an alcoholic beverage, but then to make my escape complete, I ordered a double Scotch on the rocks.

The Scotch stirred me to begin a conversation with some old guy who looked like Thurston Hall, another of my enjoyable movie character actors. The man sat across the aisle from me. He was trying to doze when I intruded.

"Excuse me, sir. I'm taking a survey. I would like to know how you would feel if you were being pursued by a young woman who looks like Hedy Lamarr."

I was delightfully surprised by his quick response and merry chuckle.

"Well, for your information, I would think I had died and gone to heaven with no possible escape from her. God, Hedy was beautiful."

A fresh-faced college kid who was reading a book on Nuclear Physics sat beside the man. He lowered the book to his lap and gazed knowingly at me.

"Aren't you Homan Kandall," he asked. "I thought I recognized you when you came on board. I'm sorry sir, but I thought you were dead. I remember when you were the best sportswriter in the state. I hope you still write."

I took another sip of my Scotch. "Thanks, son, but as you can see, I'm still draped out in this old flesh. Right now, I'm involved in a track meet. I'm trying to stay ahead of a long-striding creature who looks decidedly like Hedy Lamarr."

The old guy spoke again. "Mister, if I were you, I'd slow down and let her catch me."

The college kid said nothing more. He resumed reading about Nuclear Physics. I doubted he had much time to read sports pages, or a best-seller about unsung Hollywood heroes whose names appeared in countless movie casts. But he had been a fan of mine earlier in his life, and maybe he had the right idea. *I hope you still write.*

Okay, but what did I have to write about? Someone had already written *The Flight of the Phoenix*, and it became a suspenseful movie. I began to compare myself to that airplane. I felt like I had also crash-landed in the Sahara Desert,

That however only hounded me about what the old guy had said. I wanted no further conversation with him.

It was after nine o'clock when my changeover flight from Houston eased down at the Waco airport. I easily found my car on the nearly deserted parking lot. I pulled my glasses out of their case and slipped them over my ears. They were now a necessity for any driving I did at night.

I had to wonder what Carmela Monteza would think of that in her downplay of my alliance with reality..

Chapter Twenty
The Sermon

TWO MISERABLE WEEKS dragged their days as if heavy chains were attached to their hours. Which for me, they were.

I was despondent, lonely, and irritable. It was a sloppy, disgruntled mood that I wanted to share with no one. I even stopped having breakfast at *Denny's*. I missed the sausage and hash browns, but not Marie in her starched uniform and her homey comments. I was, I guess, afraid that in some unguarded moment I would pull her into my booth and propose marriage with orange marmalade caked on my lips.

Surely Hemingway was correct with his opinion that happiness in intelligent people is the rarest commodity that he knew. Now I had to question my intelligence which had seemingly become so flawed.

Brig's emails provided little comfort. He wrote mainly about Carmen and Carmela who were adapting to their new life at *The Beachcomber*. Being excellent cooks, they hoped to open a Mexican restaurant in Corpus. They were also fascinated by the piccolo he had given to Carmen. She wanted to take lessons and learn how to play it. Brig indicated that idea also appealed to Carmela who hoped she could have Maydell's piccolo.

It was only then that I realized I had left the instrument at *The Beachcomber*. I had left so hurriedly to avoid Carmela, I had forgotten my highly treasured possession.

Brig also informed me in his latest email that the twins were studying to take their driver's license exam. They were both good learners, he assured me. But for some obscure reason, Brig suggested nothing about me returning to Corpus Christi.

Instead of answering his letter, I placed a long distance call to *The Beachcomber*.

One of the twins answered. Hopefully, I thought it was Carmela.

"Hello, is this Carmela?"

"No, I'm her sister. Who's calling, please?"

"Carmen, this is Homan Kandall. May I speak to Carmela?"

"Wait just a moment."

It was Brig who came to the phone. "Hey Kandy, it's nice to hear from you. I thought you had become a museum piece at Baylor, maybe encased with some queen of the Nile in a mummy's slab."

His remark gave me a needed smile, but I feared he would not remain in a joking mood.

"Brig, I hope you're not still peeved about the way I left *The Beachcomber*."

"Peeved? Damn right I'm still peeved, and even more because I haven't heard from you."

"I'm calling in response to your email. Of course Carmela can have that piccolo. I phoned to tell her that. How is she?"

"She's lonely."

"She has you and Carmen."

"But Kandy, she doesn't have you, and for Carmela that's a drastic difference like night and day. It's a big sticky wad of loneliness."

I shifted in my desk chair. "I was hoping she would overcome her infatuation for me."

"Kandy, infatuation is a word Carmela doesn't know. It might as well be Greek or Latin, but I can tell you this, old stick. Carmela does know the meaning of love, a lot better than you do."

I held the phone in silence for a long, freakish moment. Finally, I resumed the conversation after shifting the phone to my other ear. I tried to be sure I said the right thing.

"Brig, I'll provide for her. I'll send her money periodically, or anything she needs. I'll help her get a college education, if that's what she wants."

His voice burst into open derision. "Oh sure, that would make everything just peaches and cream, wouldn't it? I'm thankful you didn't make that silly birdseed offer to Carmela herself. I'll just pretend I didn't hear it."

"Please let me speak to her."

"You did speak to her. That was Carmela who answered the phone. She immediately recognized your voice and pretended to be Carmen. What does that tell you, old sport?"

"Quite enough," I said lamely. I ended the conversation with a moribund promise to resume sending emails.

Another doleful week squished down the drain. But at

least the full warmth of spring refreshed my spirits. I drove out to the Baylor campus looking for anything with a cheerful tint that would relieve my sullen despair. As I passed by the university's seminary, I remembered that Geraud Collins was now a faculty member who taught Homiletics. He had come to Baylor after a long and distinguished career serving pastorates. I was certain that eventually Geraud would become dean of the Divinity School, and perhaps even president of Baylor University.

I had a sudden craving to see Geraud whom I still considered to be my brother-in-law, if only remotely. He had classes that morning, but I left word with his secretary that I would like to meet him for lunch if he were free. I suggested that he meet me at *The Grotto*, a highly visible and popular seafood restaurant near Baylor on the east bank of the Brazos River. It wasn't as famous as *The Big Fisherman* in Rockport, but it had a comparable menu that I found appealing. I was about to make my selection when Geraud strolled in.

He was still impressive looking, a man now in his sixties. His hair had not thinned, and now it was noticeably long. Geraud also wore glasses, but they did not conceal the charm of his full face. I surmised that Geraud Collins would always have the look of an eloquent Baptist preacher.

Indeed, he was still a preacher as we sat in a booth that overlooked the river. I became the recipient of his pulpit ministry. While we waited for our catfish platters, Geraud bemoaned the absence of zeal among his student preachers.

"I tell you, good buddy," he declared, "those dunderheads give me the shakes. They don't have any fire, or any style like Peter Marshall, the great Presbyterian preacher had.

THE HELPERS

From what I observe of them in the classroom, they think preaching is nothing more than shooting a few spitballs at the devil. They seem content not to rock the boat or ruffle any feathers. Their gospel is a skinny little undernourished dab of do good, feel good, and be good. I hate to think of turning them loose in any pulpit. Shoot fire, the way they omit Christ from their practice sermons, I think those people would be right at home in any synagogue."

As we dined, I briefed him on the adventuresome events that had brought Carmela Monteza and me together for the interlude that night on the veranda at *The Beachcomber.*

Geraud responded with a long, shrill whistle between bites of food.

"Heavenly days, it sounds like your Carmela did a pizzicato with your heart strings."

"Yeah, she plucked them all right."

"Well, good buddy, I think your life took a zoom like those rockets my kids work with at NASA."

"But I crashed when Carmela Monteza practically spelled out matrimony to me down there that night at Brig's home. But the fact is, I don't have any rocket fuel for a May/December marriage."

Geraud studied me intently. Under his heavy gaze, I felt like one of his spiritless classroom zombies. I knew he had some kind of sermon ready to spring on me.

"Homan, your problem is the same one you've choked on all these years. You still have Maydell imprisoned inside you. She's your captive, and you're her warden. But don't you see? She's served her sentence. It's time to turn her loose and let her spirit be forever free. Do that, and you will be free yourself.

"You think you're too old for Camela Monteza? Well, don't let your age be a dingbat crutch. So I suggest that you get your rump back down to Corpus and let Carmela breathe some new life into you. Help her to learn how to play that piccolo, but also see what lovely music you both can play together. You both have the perfect combination for it. She's young, and you're mature. You two can peel a lot of hot tamales like we did that Christmas Eve back home in Waxahachie."

Geraud was pulling out all the stops. I dared not interrupt him.

"Trust me, good buddy. The Lord is never a lame duck God. He will supply the grace for you to overcome your excuses. Like the song says, *'Then fly to her side and make her your own, or all through your life, you may dream all alone.'* You're an old movie buff, aren't you? Okay, just remember *South Pacific* and its enchanting love story. If people choose to laugh at the differences between Carmela and you, let them guffaw to high heaven. But they will find to their amazement that God never laughs at love. He's always right in the middle of its domain."

I shook hands with Geraud as we were leaving the restaurant parking lot.

"Good buddy, you're still a great preacher. Your sermon in there packed a wallop. Now I know what I must do."

"Thanks, Homan. I just hope my classroom dunces will eventually get some hot results. And hey, if you and Brigdon need someone to tie the knot with the sisters Monteza, I'll be available. Just don't ask me to throw in any Hail Marys."

That afternoon I began packing for my move to Corpus

Christi. It would require a long drive slowed by a small, rented UHaul, but I saw myself as a Roman legionnaire racing in his chariot to rescue a fair damsel from her dungeon. I knew the time spent in making the journey would be my ally. It was, after all, springtime in Texas and bluebonnets in bloom would be a spectacular sight.

I modified that thought. Bluebonnets, the state flower, would not be as spectacular as the room I now had in my heart for Carmela Monteza. Along my route to Corpus, I believed I would, in my mind, behold her in every pastoral scene, every hill and dale, and on every pleasant street corner in every town and city I passed through. In her new freedom, Maydell would be holding hands with Carmela, and together they would be waving me onward.

I'll be seeing you in all the old familiar places this heart of mine embraces. I was humming that lovely song again, and as I did, I tried to remember all of the lyrics.

Chapter Twenty One
Splendor on a Sandy Beach

TWO AFTERNOONS LATER I arrived at *The Beachcomber* without notifying Brig of the decision I had made.

So I was not surprised that no one was there when I pulled into the wide driveway. The garage door was locked, and no one answered my repeated ring of the door bell. Impatiently, I walked around the house to the steps of the veranda leading down to the beach.

I spotted one of the twins strolling along the beach at a slow, listless pace. She stopped and threw a pebble into the surf as if to indicate that it represented her vexed, despondent mood. She was barefoot and clad in blue jeans with a white shirt hanging loosely over them.

I knew at once she had to be Carmela. I quickly shook off my shoes and socks before rolling up my slacks above my ankles. My steps were a bit ponderous, but I bolted down the stairs to the beach. She still stood eyeing the bay in mystic contemplation, not realizing my presence behind her.

"Young woman, you look lonesome. May I share my life with you?" I said firmly.

Carmela wheeled around when she heard the sound of my voice. She stood frozen for a moment, apparently unsure of how to react.

I spoke again. "I am a lonely old man. I know now that I need you to add some dash and splash to my empty life. Please be my helper."

She then bounded into my arms, and I lifted her off the sandy turf with strength I did not know I possessed. I held her against my chest while kissing her with my dry, chapped lips. The embrace continued even when I eased her to the ground.

Carmela also had amazing strength, the kind she showed when she grappled with the brutish Sharonda Willis. She willfully seized my arms and yanked me off my feet. I landed on top of her, but we quickly rolled over in the sand. She rose to her knees and straddled my chest with mischievous glee.

"Now you're not a lonely old man," she laughed. "Now you're a distinguished gentleman who's learning how to live again. Now you don't have to dwell in the past. You will have me for your now and your future."

"Why didn't you talk to me when I phoned," I asked, making no effort to free myself from her bottom perched atop my chest.

"I didn't know what to say, or how to say it. Brigdon said I had a bad case of the mopes."

"The mopes are very contagious. They also infected me. But now I'm cured, thanks to Brig and a preacher friend of mine. Where are Brig and Carmen? He ought to get a picture of us lollygagging here on his beach like we're doing."

Carmela eased off, saucily pulling a sprig of my chest hair where the top of my shirt was unbuttoned. I gave her rear a playful smack in return.

"Dirty old man," she yelped. "Brigdon took her to take her driver's test. I'm supposed to take mine tomorrow, but now that you're here, I may wait awhile. You and I *padrino*, have a lot of catching up to do."

We walked along the beach, kicking sand at each other's feet. We were, for a few divine moments, unaware of anything else in the whole cockeyed, slot machine world.

At the front of Brig's cabana we paused. Carmela peered at it severely.

"That's where I almost died," she murmured.

I squeezed her hand tightly. "But you didn't die, thank God. You and Carmen survived your whole odyssey. You refused to be what I once called a tender thread that got snapped. In your fearless, gutsy way you two are survivors. Now Brig and I are going to take continual care of our twin Tondelayos. Carmela, that's not a promise. It's a proposal."

Her eyes were glary with a light I had never before seen in them.

"I accept it," she said with a broad, lingering kiss." But right now, you're too sandy. You need to take a shower in the cabana."

"You said we have a lot of catching up to do. Let's get started while you scrub my back in there."

Carmela replied by giving my rump a good, healthy boot with her bare foot.

"Dirty old man," she smiled again in mock resentment.

THE HELPERS

"Homan, that's one of those American terms Brigdon has taught Carmen and me."

"I will teach you some others."

But I knew I would not have to teach her how to kiss. She planted another wet one on my mouth as we began our walk up to *The Beachcomber*.

Thus began a period of constructive romance that shifted our thoughts away from the ominous future the Mirandez trial would bring when it finally came into the courtroom.

All of us rejoiced together that evening in hugging sprees and incessant chatter. We congratulated Carmen for passing her driver's test. She waved her temporary certificate gleefully after we dined on cold cuts and Mexican hominy for supper.

"Now I am a full-fledged citizen," she beamed.

"Tomorrow I shall accept that privilege," said Carmela.

"So Kandy, what did you and Carmela do this afternoon when you arrived," Brig said. He winked at me as he spoke. "I trust you gave her a few pointers about safe driving."

Carmela and I eyed each other with sheepish grins.

"She showed me that she is highly skilled at parking. Carmela has excellent body control. I was impressed with her coordination. I truly had a feel for her touch when she parked."

Her wide smile followed my grinning smirk.

"What Homan is trying to explain in his playful way is that I sat on his chest down on the beach. I had to be sure he didn't get away again."

"How could I? She had me pinned down, so I surrendered. I proposed to her."

"And I accepted," Carmela acknowledged as she gave me a trenchant hug.

Brig came over to shake my hand. "Man, when you finally got untracked, it was full speed ahead and damn the torpedoes. Nice going, pal, but what an idiotic way to get engaged."

"Well maybe so, but I didn't want to swindle any more time away from us. Now I've got to make it official by slipping an engagement ring on Carmela's finger like the one you have, Carmen. That should get all of us squared away, at least for the respectable now."

"The sooner the better," Carmen said as she gave me a lively kiss. "Okay, when shall we do the wedding scene?"

It was a question whose answer did not come quickly. The stigma of the Mirandez trial and our participation in it still hung heavy over us. That became a decided factor in our conversation that evening. So were the twins' piccolo lessons and their fervent hope to open a Mexican restaurant. Brig and I had no qualms about the venture. We knew their culinary talents would make it a profitable enterprise.

"Here's my suggestion," I said at last. "Let's aim for a June double wedding in Waco. I think you ladies would enjoy seeing Baylor and getting married there."

"We've heard about this Baylor," said Carmen. "What is Baylor?"

"It's a university in Waco," said Brig. "Kandy and I graduated from Baylor way back in 1950."

Carmela's eyes widened with curiosity. "Do they play football there? Carmen and I have always wanted to see an American football game. It must be a lot different from the *futbol* they play in Mexico. That is, when they're not busy bull-fighting."

THE HELPERS

"Yeah sweetheart, Baylor plays football, but not very well most of the time. But if you and Carmen can put up with us old dudes in marriage, you ought to be able to survive a Baylor football game. Brig and I will take you to a game up there."

Late into the evening we were still mapping out our future plans. Carmen then suggested that we shove them aside and have some fun playing games.

I accepted the idea even though I detested a lot of games. But I was agreeable to anything that would prolong my evening with Carmela.

Brig also nodded his agreement. "All right, how about a game of *Scrabble*? Kandy, I've been helping the girls learn new words with it."

"Carmela used some of them this afternoon on the beach," I laughed.

She rejected Brig's choice with a mischievous chuckle.

"Scrabble is much too tame, *mi companero*. For a night like this, we need to do something exciting. How about a game of strip poker? Carmen and I will play you guys."

Brig and I looked at each other with smug satisfaction. He and I had played a lot of poker during World War Two and a few times at Baylor. We could not even remotely imagine the Monteza twins having any chance of keeping their clothes on against us.

I turned to Carmela. "Honey, Brig and I know all about poker. We would be taking a terrible advantage of you and Carmen. That wouldn't be fair. It would be uncivilized and indecent."

"You think so? Brigdon, just get the cards. We'll see

who's left sitting around in their skivvies. That's what you call your drawers, isn't it?"

While we munched popcorn, the game quickly turned one-sided. Brig and I began giving ourselves stupefying looks when we lost several hands and had to peel off articles of our clothing. The strip fest began with our shoes and socks. Then when Carmela drew an inside straight, we had nothing left on but our under shorts. The rest of our clothes lay crumpled in a heap on the floor. We again eyed each other in complete bewilderment. In all their escapades, Laurel and Hardy never looked more pathetic.

With a surreal impersonation of Oliver Hardy, I said to Brig, "Well, here's another nice mess you got us into."

I was thankful that Brig didn't start blubbering like Stan Laurel always did when doused with blame from his demeaning partner.

The women began laughing at our predicament.

"Fellows, you've suffered enough," said Carmen. "We won't ask you to shed what's left of your modesty. We might even let you win the next time, after we're married, of course."

Carmen kept stroking the deck of cards like one of those old riverboat gamblers on the Mississippi. She and Carmela shook their heads in mock sorrow at our hapless plight.

Carmela finally relented, knowing that Brig and I needed some kind of explanation about how well she and Carmen played poker.

"You don't have to look so sad about losing your pants," she smiled. "Carmen and I were forced to play strip poker when the cartel held us captive in *Nuevo Laredo*. We lost everything to those *bastardos* every time they made us play.

THE HELPERS

They exploited us, but we learned all about strip poker from them."

Despite the hideous outcome of the poker game, I again marveled at the amazing gumption of the twins. They were resourceful, resilient, and vigilant survivors who knew how to triumph over torment and degradation.

Little wonder then that Brig and I could not match their poker skills. But all that also assured me that when adversity came along, the Monteza sisters would be wives who could chortle at its numbing gestures with thumbs to their noses. That was part of their bravado fiber, and it showed in their compelling sense of humor. It was the solid ground of matrimonial longevity.

I gave Brig a gentle pat on his arm. "We got plucked by a couple of sharpies, old stick. But that's okay. These ladies gave us something in return. They snatched our clothes, but they draped us in the mantle of camaraderie that will add the sauce of catnip, the bubbly of champagne, the flame of Cherries Jubilee, and the sweep of the tango to our lives."

Carmen had a question for Brig. "What's he talking about?"

"My wordsmith friend is saying that caring is sharing. It is a term that has been with us for a pile of years. Homan and I don't think it's ready for moth balls. We want it to stay in circulation during our married years."

Brig and I didn't bother to get dressed. We picked up the wad of our clothes and shuffled out of the den like two naughty little boys being sent to their room for dreadful misbehavior. Nonetheless, as I left I could not resist giving the twins a defiant shake of my rear end.

WILLIAM HORICK

They returned my impudent gesture with the old wolf whistle.

"Caring is sharing," I heard Carmela say.

Or was it Maydell that I heard? I knew in spirit she was present, enjoying the role that Carmela now played in the revolving door of our human comedy.

Chapter Twenty Two
Ambrosia Days

WE WAITED IMPATINETLY for the Mirandez trial to begin.

The state of Texas had an airtight case against him for the murder of Judge Roy Davlin and the attempted murder of the twins. But the U.S. system of justice got caught in the rigmarole of an international relationship with Mexico. The feds on both sides of the Rio Grande wanted to prosecute Mirandez as a drug baron, hoping to scuttle his far-flung cartel. Carmen and Carmela were the key witnesses because they alone would willingly supply helpful information about his base of operations.

While both sides haggled over jurisdiction, Brig and I continued to live with two beautiful women without the benefit of clergy. That may have bothered a few gossipy tongues in the neighborhood, but not us. It was strictly a platonic arrangement. For our part, we continually observed proper decorum. Carmela and Carmen expected no sexual advances from us, and we offered them none. They became, once more, our *daughters*. Our love for them widened each day, but it was a love that knew its boundaries. In observance of those physical limitations, we dared not risk the lark of another game of strip poker. Our respective in-house engagements played the waiting game to the hilt while we bowed to abstinence. To outsiders, it might have seemed to be something right out of *The Twilight Zone* with all of its weird characters, but I thought Rod Serling would understand.

We knew, of course, that as potential witnesses against Mirandez we were under constant surveillance by the feds. Those guard dogs were inconspicuous, but we were not free to travel anywhere without their company. Even with Mirandez in custody, we knew the cartel remained a threat to our lives.

Still, that waiting period became ambrosia days for all of us. *The Beachcomber* became not a love nest, but a happy place of contentment and courtesy as we watched our appreciation for each other grow significantly every blessed day.

The twins played their piccolos daily, their skill always on the upswing. Sour notes became a rarity. They also learned more idioms of the English language and facets of American slang. Throughout their learning process, Carmen and Carmela thanked their tutors with fabulous meals.

"You can be our publicity agents when we open a Mexican restaurant," Carmen told us after a lavish dinner.

Brig rubbed his stomach with a sigh. "Just keep feeding Kandy and me like you've been doing and you'll have the best ad men imaginable. You will never need Madison Avenue."

Carmela, however, wanted something more than publicity or a clientele for a restaurant that remained a nebulous idea at best. She spoke to me one day on the veranda about her passion to write.

THE HELPERS

"Homan, you're a writer. I want you to teach me how to spin words onto paper. I want to describe what life is all about in its noblest sense. Carmen and I have experienced the bitterness and the ugly face it springs on people, but I want to tell everyone how they need to seek and find its beauty. Please say you will help me to do that."

I placed my arm around her slender waist.

"Sweetheart, of course I'll help you to find that side of life. We'll live it together during the allotment of time I still have on earth. I won't sling a lot of words at you for you to write, but in time you will find a proper way to express your thoughts clearly and precisely, and I hope to be around when you do."

"Shame on you, Homan. You're beginning to sound like an old man again. You're not an old man. I didn't fall in love with an old man. How often must I keep reminding you of that?"

I tightened my hold on her. Carmela in turn kissed me with her usual display of passion. Locked to each other, I knew I was not feeling my age in that delicious moment. But still, I knew I had to reach back for at least a sip of realism again.

"Carmela, I'm nearly seventy-three years old. I'm old enough to be your grandfather. That's not something I'm just saying. A lot of old jokers have said something like that to much younger women. It's always trite, but they still say it, and I had to say it just now, because trite or not, it is also true."

"But you're not my grandfather, *mi corazon dulce*. You're the man I'm going to marry. Like that saying I've learned from you---come hell or high water."

My gentle laughter caught her by surprise.

"Kiddo, you sound just like Maydell, the wife I had a long time ago. Let me tell you something about her. You have her same spirited, animated approach to life. She had a daredevil streak in her that I also have detected in you. She didn't play footsy with old standards or hackneyed traditions. She had a pioneer's zeal to explore new horizons. Carmela, you are very much like her."

"And you still miss her, don't you? I hope that some day after we marry, you will let me genuinely take her place."

"I want to be completely honest with you, Carmela. You may never be able to take her place fully or completely," I said pensively. "Maydell was pregnant when she was killed. At my age, I can't promise you a pregnancy or even much of a sex life."

Carmela kissed me again. Once more she felt my masculine impulse come to life. She laughed, knowing that she had caused me to have that modest physical upsurge.

"Oh no?", she smiled. "That wasn't exactly foam rubber that I felt pressed against my loins just now."

"Confound it, Carmela, that sounds exactly like something Maydell would say."

"That's fine. I like the comparison. So let me become her in the fullest measure possible. And please understand that I don't want to be that Hedy Lamarr I've heard you talk about so often. She had her place on a movie screen. My place is with you. I just want to be the woman you love, even if I have to keep sharing you with your Maydell."

A swath of foamy Gulf clouds brought a sudden downpour. Carmela and I did not mind those raindrops with their sweet spring fragrance. They did not dislodge our embrace, but served instead to linger our stay on the veranda. As we did, her wet blouse showed proof of her throbbing womanhood.

I had to believe those federal agents watching us, wherever they were, got a lusty eyeful in their vigilant spyglass lenses.

When we finally ducked inside the den, Carmela and I both were confident our sexuality would pose no problems in our marriage, nor would my memory of Maydell.

Brig, on the other hand, never detailed his thoughts about Freddie Foster to Carmen. He had occasionally talked about her to me, but I knew that for Brigdon Chonliff, Freddie had become just an interlude in his past. He had loved her fiercely, but now he was ready to begin a new chapter, the final chapter of his life, with Carmen Monteza, whatever the script might be.

"Inside the sack or outside the sack won't matter," he told me one morning. "I will love Carmen poignantly, regardless of how I perform in bed. That doesn't bother her. She knows I've never been married. You know what she said when I reminded her of that? She just laughed that throaty little laugh of hers. She said, 'Well dearest, that makes us even. Neither have I'".

With each passing day, the four of us became more antsy about the delay of our double wedding. I had to call Geraud Collins and ask him to keep his schedule flexible. We were also dreading the Mirandez trial, especially since the venue had been moved to Brownsville at the insistence of the federal government.

Chapter Twenty Three
Questions and Answers

THE MIRANDEZ TRIAL lasted nearly three weeks. We felt emotionally drained when it was finally over. The twins furnished most of the testimony for the prosecution as expected, and it was damnable to the cruel-eyed, swarthy defendant. They had to endure his relentless scorn during their time on the witness stand, but they never wavered from openly revealing the severity of their treatment while captives of the cartel for three miserable years of degradation. Carmela even showed the court the crease on her forehead that Mirandez had caused.

The Monteza sisters also gave lengthy statements about their escape and its harrowing route to Corpus Christi where they finally found refuge at *The Beachcomber*. The defense attorney wanted them barred from the case, citing the rat poisoning and public trespassing, but he was quickly overruled by the judge who knew no charges would be brought against them.

Those druggies, Maclard and Willis, had also delayed the start of the trial. They requested and were granted a jail cell wedding in return for relating how Mirandez had plotted to kill the twins at *The Beachcomber*. As husband and wife in custody they were a pathetic looking sight in the courtroom, but the hulking Sharonda Willis added a bit of comic relief to the trial.

"I should have held out for a church wedding," we heard her lament in her testimony. She also scolded herself for not pursuing a Hollywood movie career. "I could have been a bigger star than that Bette Davis."

Brig and I also testified about the visit with Judge Davlin and the blotched murder attempt at *The Beachcomber* with the poisoned hamburgers. Detective Tony Delgado testified how the police intercepted the deliveryman which in turn led to the trap that was sprung on Mirandez as he approached *The Beachcomber*.

As the trial continued, the newshounds turned it into a courtroom spectacle. Each day cameras flashed in our faces, both inside and outside the courtroom. All the TV networks stormed into Brownsville, the picturesque and historic city with its bevy of *resacas* at the tip end of Texas. They were determined to provide their newscasts with ample, intricate details about the people involved in the drama.

Those news hawks especially found Brig and me worthy of their attention. They lavishly told their audiences about how two old Baylor grads got involved with two young women who both looked like Hedy Lamarr. They even produced old movie stills of Hedy to verify the resemblance.

We tried to relax during those interviews, but both Brig and I knew that like it or not, we were now national celebrities. Regretfully, I drew the bulk of attention because I was a well-known sportswriter and author. The publicity we got also vaulted Baylor University into the limelight, and I had to wonder how its administration felt about that recognition. Brig and I could only hope that the madcap media would soon stumble across some hot late-breaking story that would eclipse the trial. We felt it would take that kind of news to get the media phalanx off our backs.

Brig had a chilling suggestion. "How about a mass evacuation of the Waldorf Astoria caused by a deadly king cobra some nutty, revenge-minded former employee turned loose somewhere inside. That panic would ease us out of the picture."

"Very creepy, and I hate snakes," I replied. "But it might take something really gory, maybe a terrorist attack with car bomb explosions on the Golden Gate Bridge in the middle of rush hour traffic."

We waited hopefully each day for our redemption, but it never emerged.

Someone from ABC had the gall to ask us if we felt romantically inclined toward Carmen and Carmela Monteza. The reporter thought the question would simply add a nice juicy twist to the trial and the sideshow it provoked. He nearly swallowed his microphone when I answered his question.

"Romantically inclined? Yes, I think that's true if you define our upcoming double wedding as being romantically inclined."

My sarcastic comment sent the media spewing into a new frenzy as it sought additional tidbits to feed the public. Predictably, they began calling *The Beachcomber* a love port.

THE HELPERS

Brig finally berated a reporter for that falsehood. "How could it be a love port? The girls are too busy taking piccolo lessons day and night."

That opened a new jar of hot sauce for the media mullets who now buzzed around us like a swarm of gnats. Their questions ranged from the absurd to the nonsensical and always in league with the outlandish.

What piccolos and how did the Monteza sisters obtain them?

Oh, so they formerly belonged to your lady friends who played them in the Baylor University band?

Well, that had to be a long time ago, didn't it? How playable were the piccolos after all those years?

Do you still have any Baylor pictures of those girls when they played in the band?

How did this Baptist preacher become involved?

Pardon me. Did we hear you correctly, Mr. Kandall? He was your brother-in-law, and now he's going to officiate at your double wedding?

And you say the two of you had fun peeling hot tamales one Christmas Eve?

We answered such questions as quickly and courteously as we possibly could during the trauma of the trial. But it was a college intern who finally soured our patience. He caught us off guard even though we should have expected something so gross. Time, after all, had brought the country near to the end of the zany 20th century that accepted as normal a clatter for the ridiculous and obscene.

The intern put the squeeze on us poolside at the hotel where we were staying during the trial.

"Guys, just tell me one thing, off the record, of course.

How do you old farts like that Mexican hot stuff? Aren't those two jalapeno peppers more than you can handle?"

"Son, they're more than you could handle," Brig snapped.

"They're your playthings, not mine," the intern retorted.

"Young man, why don't you find a job with *Playboy Magazine*", I fired back. "You talk like you're tailor-made for it. But for your sordid information, the Monteza sisters are American citizens. You're forgetting their nationality was established early in the trial."

"They still sounded like hot-blooded, horny Mexican senoritas in the courtroom, the way they kept looking at you with those bedroom eyes of theirs when they spoke."

"And you sound like Donald Duck the way you're quacking," said Brig with a pale smile. "Now be a real duck and take a swim."

With those words, Brig shoved our inquisitor into the pool. That of course ended the interview. But it also got us entangled with more unwanted publicity.

The trial also ended, much to our relief. After little deliberation, the jury returned to the courtroom with the expected verdict. Mirandez, still sinister looking, stood and heard that he was guilty of capital murder for the slaying of Judge Roy Davlin. The jurors also recommended a life sentence for him with no possibility of a parole. We were satisfied with the verdict, but as Mirandez was led away, I remembered Alonzo Pereida. It had been some drug baron, perhaps Mirandez, who indirectly caused him to kill Maydell and the life in her womb. I did not say *lo siento* to Mirandez at the end of his trial.

Mirandez never served a day of his sentence. As he was

THE HELPERS

escorted away outside the courtroom, an assailant fired several bullets into his chest and somehow eluded the cordon of police officers. We heard about this disturbing twist to the Mirandez trial from Detective Tony Delgado.

Tony informed us that the gunman likely was a paid killer another cartel had hired. He believed it may have been an act of revenge even though Mirandez had been convicted and was out of circulation.

"The conviction wouldn't matter to the rival cartel. Killings are commonplace with those people. That's the way they operate to stay in business," he said. "They clash with each other in the traffic, so they're ready to gun down any opposition they may have encountered. Those people, as you already know, have a very low regard for human life, especially if someone horns in on their side of the street, or in the case of Mirandez, their side of the Rio Grande."

Carmen and Carmela were relieved that Mirandez was dead. They were edgy about the verdict, fearing that he would somehow escape and track them down again.

"You're safe now," Tony told them. "I don't think the other cartels will bother you. They're just happy you helped smash the Mirandez ring. Now he's a dead rat, and the overlords are thankful he won't be after a slice of their melon any longer."

"That's good news," said Carmela. "My sister and I have a lot of living and loving to do with our guys. We're going to start a new life with them, and we'll put the pox on anybody who says we shouldn't."

"You will have the full support of the Rockport Police Department," Tony laughed. "Carmela, just don't make a spectacle of yourself again at *The Big Fisherman*. You might start a riot."

"I'll see that she behaves," I promised. "She will be too involved with me in a personal project to pull another stunt like that."

Carmela's eyes popped wide with fond expectation. "Do you mean something for just the two of us?"

"That's right. I think you and I should stay busy writing sugary poetry to each other like Robert and Elizabeth Barrett Browning once did."

"Why of course," Brig sighed with a smile. "And that endearing little gambit could create shockwaves as modern English Lit. You could demand a new wing for the Armstrong-Browning Library at Baylor. So I say, why not? Everything goes modern sooner or later. Even English Lit needs to get out of its musty old pages and into the word wear of today."

"But not too drastically, I hope," I said. "Classics must always remain classics, however ingenious their shuffle may be."

"Homan, let's create a new classic and share it with the world."

Carmela was smiling when she spoke, but I knew she was raptly serious.

We said goodbye to Detective Tony Delgado, but not to the idea of touring the famous library which added such a magnificent luster to the Baylor campus.

Brig and I promised the twins we would tour the library during our honeymoon in Waco. Like the Texas Ranger Museum close to the campus on the Brazos, the library was a major tourist attraction.

THE HELPERS

"Will we see pictures of Hedy Lamarr at the library," Carmen asked naively.

"I hardly think so," I replied with a grin. "But you and Carmela will be on display there. You will be love sonnets that stand out much more than any Browning poetry. And believe me, that's a supreme compliment to you both."

With the katzenjammer disruption of the Mirandez trial now gone, all of us savored our wedding trip to Waco, regardless of what the Armstrong-Browning Library had to offer us as honeymooners.

We set a date for our double wedding after we returned to *The Beachcomber*. We chose June 6th because it was a very significant day in history. Carmela and Carmen wanted to be June brides, and Brig and I felt that if we still remembered the date of the Normandy invasion in 1944, we could also, at our advanced age, remember our wedding anniversary.

But we didn't know if our own invasion on the night of June 6th would produce any cannon salvo. We told each other that our young brides might have to settle for blank cartridges.

Chapter Twenty Four
Coming Attractions

GERAUD COLLINS met us at *The Grotto* for what was supposed to be a wedding rehearsal dinner.

But he was so stunned by the Monteza sisters' elegant beauty, Geraud said very little about the double ceremony until we finished our meal in a private sector of the restaurant.

I tried to downplay the attention he poured on them.

"Girls, don't be alarmed by the attentive stares the Reverend Dr. Collins keeps bestowing on you. He is a worthy man of the cloth. He's had a cloistered career, but you fascinate him with your Hedy Lamarr looks, although I'm quite sure he's never even seen a Hedy Lamarr movie."

"Not true, Homan, good buddy", Geraud replied. "Strictly in the interest of biblical accuracy you must understand, I saw Hedy in *Samson And Delilah* on TCM. That vixen fogged up my glasses the way she kept pestering poor old Samson to reveal the source of his strength. When he finally did, she clipped his locks and he became a pathetic weakling. Then the Philistines pounced on him. My friends, hear me good. I'll never get a haircut from a lady barber. I've got my own Philistines to worry about."

Carmela smiled and looked at Geraud's impressive hairstyle. "Sir, suppose I was a lady barber. Wouldn't you trust me with that magnificent mop of hair you have?"

We laughed at her pert remark, and waited for Geraud to make one of his noted comebacks. But he simply joined our laughter as he looked fondly at both Carmela and Carmen before he spoke again.

"Say, I like your moxie even though it momentarily caught me off guard," he said. "But that happens to all people, even preachers. The key is learning how to rebound. That's a good tonic for any married couple, as you four people will truly discover in your respective marriages. You must not allow some rampageous event or person to push you into any garbage can of despair. You cannot allow yourselves to wallow in that stench. You must put up your dukes and come back swinging with your heads held up high."

That was the core of Geraud's pre-wedding counsel to us. I knew, however, that he would have to mention our religious beliefs, which he did.

"Carmen and Carmela, I assume you are Catholics."

"No sir, that's not exactly true," said Carmen. "We were baptized into the Church as infants. We have a record of that. But neither of us ever truly embraced the faith, especially after our parents were killed. Oh, there was the time we hid in a convent when the Mirandez thugs came looking for us. The Sisters disguised us as nuns. But we got thrown into a lot of garbage cans, like you said. We didn't find any religion there."

"But God took care of you," said Geraud.

"We had to take care of ourselves," Carmen replied rather crisply.

Her statement was blunt and to the point. Brig and I knew the Monteza sisters were not agnostics. But we hoped that Geraud Collins, the highly skilled man of God, could appreciate their lack of theological truisms. They had put up their mitts and fought like wildcats to stay alive as they fled from the slavery of the Mirandez drug cartel. At times they had resorted to trickery and deception to secure their freedom like they did at the convent. Brig and I also knew that Geraud was correct. God did take care of them in His mysterious way. But we were glad Geraud wisely did not choose to press them about their religion.

Carmela had her own opinion about the meaning of care.

"Reverend Collins, our knowledge of faith is limited. But we do believe that God led us to Brigdon Chonliff and Homan Kandall. They took care of us, and from them Carmen and I have learned what Christianity is really all about. It's about loving people and helping them in their distress. That's what our marriage to them will always include."

Geraud accepted her declaration as a genuine and practical profession of faith. He flashed a broad smile that revealed his pure delight with her credo.

"Well spoken, my dear. I know now that I won't have to preach you ladies into your wedding tomorrow."

Carmela appended her vow. "Sir, we'll go wherever our husbands go, and our lives will mesh with theirs. Carmen and I will honor that union with religious faith and trust. We will strengthen each other's citizenship in doing that.

THE HELPERS

Homan and Brigdon are Texans, and we want to be Texans with them. Sir, does that sound...what's the word...corny?"

Geraud patted her hand. "No, it absolutely does not. Quite the contrary, it sounds exactly like what's written in the Old Testament Book of Ruth."

We sat there at our table overlooking the Brazos River, suddenly mindful that we were the last customers in *The Grotto*. Surprisingly, the patronage had been light the entire evening.

Geraud furnished a startling bit of information as we prepared to leave.

"This was a great place for our meeting, my friends, but you may not be dining here again. You're probably aren't aware that *The Grotto* is pulling up its fishing nets. The place is closing at the end of this month."

The twins eyed each other with sudden affirmative glances. Clearly, their thoughts shared a common pipeline that blended with the idea that life is more than a bowl of cherries. Life for them was a heaping bowl of corn chips siding up to a platter of tamales, enchiladas, and tacos with chili gravy, rice and beans. That was the shibboleth of the Tex Mex restaurant they had begun to crave.

"Will it be available as another restaurant," asked Carmen.

"It could be a very tough act for someone to follow," said Geraud. "But yes, I wouldn't expect this property to remain vacant very long."

Brig and I became energized as instant mind-readers. We knew what the girls were thinking on the eve of their wedding. He voiced our mutual thoughts.

"You want this to be the Mexican restaurant you've been

talking about, don't you?" he smiled.

"Can we do it", asked Carmela as she latched tightly onto my arm. "It can be our wedding present to each other."

Brig made no attempt to discourage the idea, giving her a wink.

"Well, if you want to be Texans, there's no better way to start than by owning a Mexican restaurant. Just don't overlook the *chili con queso* or the pecan pralines. And it might not hurt to include a juicy Texas steak somewhere in the menu."

"We'll have to float a very large loan," I said as I curled into the recidivism of reality once again.

"That should be easy enough," Geraud stated. "After that trial, you people are now celebs. You have developed clout down at the state legislature in Austin. Yeah, and the Longhorn Band has even played the UT *alma mater* down there in your honor. The eyes of Texas are indeed upon you. Not to be upstaged, Texas A&M now wants to make you honorary Aggies at a football game this fall. And for good measure, I will put in a strong recommendation for you with the Lord. Oh, by the way, I have heard on campus that Baylor is now planning to honor you in its Homecoming in October. I have also heard that *Texas Monthly* will do a big spread about you.

"But first things first," Geraud continued. "Now get ready to savor your private wedding tomorrow afternoon. I fear your lives won't be very private afterwards. Accept all those plaudits you get, but spurn the offers to endorse certain products that feature a lot of commercial chicanery. Shoot, you'll probably be guests on the David Letterman show. You will enjoy that, but please don't sacrifice your dignity as an offshoot."

We thanked Geraud for his advice as we left *The Grotto*. Brig and I were glad to get back to our downtown hotel. It had been a busy and tiring day for us old geezers, and our wedding day was still to come. In our hotel room, we both conked out before the 10 o'clock news on TV.

He and I vowed that we would not succumb to sleep so early tomorrow night when our wives would be at our side. But I wasn't so sure. Old geezer routines are hard to break, I reasoned.

Even when you're in bed with a wife who looks like Hedy Lamarr.

Chapter Twenty Five
Dearly Beloved

OUR WEDDING HOUR logged in at two o'clock the next afternoon.

Brig and I stood at the altar in the Baylor chapel with Geraud Collins in front of us as we awaited the entrance of Carmen and Carmela. A student organist softly played the prelude. The small congregation consisted of a few Divinity students Geraud had rounded up to witness the ceremony.

We bridegrooms wore dark tuxedo trousers and white dinner jackets with red boutonnieres. We looked like a couple of over-aged Dapper Dans whose nerves were beginning to unravel.

"At ease, good buddies," Geraud cautioned. "Just relax. This is your wedding, not a confrontation with the IRS." He looked resplendent in a white suit with a red carnation attached to his coat.

I tried to smile. I again saw Geraud as Maydell's kid brother, the little sprig who had popped out of the cocoon of his childhood and into the elect ranks of ordained clergy. It had been a grand transformation, I knew. Geraud would

THE HELPERS

tie a good, solid matrimonial knot. That however did not relieve the tension starting to flare within me.

The student organist ended her prelude and smoothly segued into the strains of *The Wedding March*. Brig and I turned to watch the approach of our brides down the aisle. Carmen and Carmela strolled slowly toward us holding hands. They wore pale blue dresses, having shunned the traditional white wedding gowns out of deference to their background as captives of Mirandez and his henchmen. That decision did not matter to Brig and me. All we actually observed was the radiant purity in their faces as they approached. They had been to a beauty parlor that morning, and the bouffant of their dark hair sparkled like diadems in a splendor that augmented the glow of their luxurious smiles as they took our arms.

Geraud began the ceremony with the traditional opening phrase.

"Dearly Beloved, we are gathered here. . ." But he suddenly paused and looked sternly at his invited witnesses.

"No, that's incorrect. You student people will only become dearly beloved when you learn how to preach the gospel Word with zeal and dispatch. But today you are here to observe a unique double wedding, and I trust it shall provide you with inspiration for a future sermon. Rest assured, this is no slapdash ceremony uniting two mismatched couples. You instead are witness to a love that transcends age and background. You are seeing how genuine respect and resolve can fashion four lives into a loving matrimonial state with the blessings of Almighty God. Therefore, I urge you to have only supreme, wholesome thoughts about this ceremony which must be regarded as a time of holy worship. I am conducting this service, but you must understand that God arranged it."

After that thunderbolt charge, Geraud centered his attention on us with the standard wedding ritual, and we made our appropriate response.

"I Brigdon take thee Carmen. . "

"I Homan take thee Carmela. . ."

Brig and I placed our wedding rings on the fingers of our brides, and with them we continued our respective vows. Then we knelt as Geraud blest us with his bestowal of Divine grace. After those words, Brig and I were able to stand again, amazingly without anyone's aid.

Suddenly with a modicum of organ fanfare, those old codgers, Brigdon Chonliff and Homan Kandall were properly married to the starry-eyed Monteza twins amid the applause of the student onlookers.

Geraud, as expected, had the final word. He supplied a rousing benediction.

"Now gentlemen, you may kiss your lovely brides. Then go with them out into society to celebrate the holy gift your Divine Father has given you. In all that you do, be faithful to Him and to each other all through your lives. Amen."

We raced out of the chapel, expecting to make a quick, clean getaway. Instead, we came face to face with a posse of media people. Cameras flashed as questioners squeezed around us. A shower of rice would have been preferable, but we somehow were able to plunge through the knot of interrogators, smiling broadly but offering no answers for their disgusting quiz show. We piled into a rented limo driven

THE HELPERS

by a young man named Bryce whom Geraud had selected to haul us away from the chapel. Bryce, we learned, was a recent seminary grad who had made Geraud's dearly beloved team.

Bryce courteously drove us to our downtown hotel, choosing not to observe our happy marital melee in the backseats of the car where Carmen and Carmela frolicked on our laps. At the hotel Brig and I both tipped him generously. We added our hope that he would have great success as a Baptist preacher.

"Thank you," Bryce smiled. "But I'm a Methodist who somehow got accepted by Baylor. Perhaps I'll see you in church someday. I would be honored to have you in my congregation."

"I'm glad old Baylor has gone ecumenical," Brig said.

"Why not," Bryce replied. "There's a lot of ecumenicity now, especially in weddings, and you folks vindicate its meaning. Congratulations."

We caught the slant of his remark and laughed.

"Young man, you're very perceptive," I remarked. "You sound like an embryo bishop."

Bryce smiled again. "Thanks for the compliment, but I'll settle to be like your friend, Dr. Collins."

"Get him, sometime, to tell you about the sight he had of his sister when he was a nine year old kid," I suggested.

The twins knew the story. Perhaps that's why they quickly herded their husbands into the hotel away from Bryce.

Brig and I congratulated each other in the lobby while Carmela and Carmen posed for pictures with the mayor of Waco.

"Kandy, that old axiom remains true, doesn't it, that old dogs still have their day?"

"Let's just hope they also still have their nights," I responded with a friendly tap on Brig's chest.

He gave me a brisk salute. "Even after all these years, I see that you still have your subtle humor."

I awoke the next morning with Carmela curled up beside me on our bed. My pajama top was loosely draped over a nearby chair in our hotel room. Only when I answered her kiss did I became aware that she was already fully dressed and ready to serve me the breakfast she had ordered from Room Service.

I roused up, expecting her to place the food tray across my body. But instead, she playfully sprinkled my chest with drops of ice water from a champagne bucket on a light stand near the head of our bed.

The impact made me jump.

"You also jumped last night, my love. I made you jump real good."

"Was I good?"

Carmela swept away the cold spot on my chest with her tongue.

"You probed me with gentleness. You gave me your full self, but without any wild exploitation. Homan, my dearest, I don't give a hoot about how you regard your age. I only know you're the absolute man that I'm proud to have as my husband."

She and I spent most of the day with Carmen and Brig exploring the sights of Waco. We saved the best until late

THE HELPERS

that afternoon when we drove through the sylvan hills of Cameron Park. We stopped finally at Lover's Leap, the highest point of elevation in the city. Brig and I had been there before with Maydell and Freddie, but they were only girl friends on a date.

Now we had brand new wives, charmingly inquisitive and exciting, and they added spice to the rugged grandeur of the jagged cliff where we stood. We gazed out at the panoramic view of the distant countryside, while deeply impressed by the lazy Bosque River below. A short distance downstream, its mouth breathed more life into the Brazos as a faithful tributary.

"We'll come here again, won't we," Carmela asked hopefully.

I agreed with a momentary nod. "Sure, if we can find the time. Our restaurant business will keep us awfully busy, you know."

"But not too busy when we have some great moments that can only be shared here in all this beauty, I hope," said Carmela.

Brig took Carmen to another vantage point at the edge of Lover's Leap. He stood there, apparently lost in contemplation. His face showed a high touch of inspiration when he stepped back from the perilous bluff with Carmen.

"Let's call our restaurant the *Dos Piccolos*," he suggested. "That will be a vague remembrance of those earlier years, but more so now as a tribute to Carmen and Carmela. Ladies, you have brought new life to those old musical instruments and to Homan and me as well."

Carmen enthusiastically put her arm around Brig in ready agreement with his idea.

"We'll play them at *Dos Piccolos* during the dinner hours," she purred. "We'll also have *senoritas* twirling their bright colored skirts while they click castanets."

She did a hasty impromptu demonstration of her vision.

"And strolling troubadours in Mexican sombreros entertaining customers with guitars and maracas as a mariachi band," Carmela beamed. "Our customers will enjoy all that while they dine."

"What, no strip tease," I joked.

We left Lover's Leap, but our enthusiasm for the future *Dos Piccolos* dominated our honeymoon stay in Waco. Oh sure, we toured the Baylor campus, and visited the Texas Ranger Museum. We also went boating on Lake Waco, and we saw a musical at the civic theatre one evening after we had an immodest dinner at *The Olive Garden*. Carmela and Carmen of course did a lot of shopping, as wives are wont to do. But during those salad days, our collective minds were always focused on the restaurant. We consulted people and made inquiries at *The Grotto*.

Finally however, we settled back into the stern realization that we would have to move from Corpus Christi. That would be no profound upheaval for the twins and me. But for Brig it would be a drastic change that would require a sad farewell to his beloved *Beachcomber* with its bayside intrigue. Double C had been his home since 1950, and he was well-established there with his photography and high respectability as one of the city's leading citizens.

Carmela and I discussed the matter privately. We agreed the change could be a shaky venture for Brig at his age, and we wondered if he would accept the challenge. After all, we

THE HELPERS

reasoned, *Dos Piccolos* could be based in Corpus Christi, thus eliminating any fretful shuffle up to Waco. We agreed that whatever Brig decided, we would ratify with our mutual accord. We knew our love for him would accept nothing less.

Chapter Twenty Six
Dos Piccolos

Our honeymoon spiral continued in undeterred merriment. Each day we continued to live and love, shoving the big decision aside in our marital gaiety. It was not until the morning of our last day that Brig shared his thoughts about *Dos Piccolos* with us.

He had hinted that he would the night before when all of us were splashing around in the hotel pool after hours when the pool was supposed to be vacated.

It was one of those warm Texas nights, prodding the water to refresh and relax our bodies. The twins looked finely honed and svelte in their swimsuits when they climbed out of the pool. Brig helped Carmen dry off, an obvious pleasant task for him.

"Tomorrow will be a special day for all of us," he said. "But now it's late, and nearly bedtime."

"Yes, definitely bedtime," Carmen laughed as he toweled her lower back.

We were having breakfast in the hotel coffee shop when Brig announced his preference for the location of *Dos Piccolos*.

THE HELPERS

He was firmly holding Carmen's hand when he spoke. His voice carried no timorous undertone.

"Kandy, you and I met here in Waco at Baylor. This is where I quit chasing women, and met my first true love. We graduated from Baylor, and we have been attracted, in some way, to the old school ever since. Not always directly, perhaps. But it is still *Alma Mater,* and I want Carmen to understand what Baylor is, and what it represents. It's a love affair, like the one I have for her."

Carmen squeezed his hand as she tugged it to her lips.

"Sweetheart, I want us both to be close to Baylor's pulse and heartbeat," Brig continued. "As your husband, I want to be a grateful alumnus who has something to give back to the university."

Brig turned to Carmela and me. "Kandy, you and I have our BA degrees. But now with our brand new wives, we're going to get a different kind of education. I believe that education should begin right across the Brazos where *Dos Piccolos* absolutely must be located. That's a perfect location for us. Therefore, I propose that we move ahead with our original idea and plant our flag over there at *The Grotto.* We'll do it with love and respect, each of us sharing those vital elements with one another here in this old overgrown cotton town the Huaco Indians founded a long time ago."

I stood up with a glass of orange juice in my hand.

"Brigdon, let's all drink to that. Let's clink our glasses in a toast to the four of us, not only in our business endeavor, but also in the venture of marriage for the remainder of our lives whatever the longevity they may hold."

Other diners in the coffee shop halted their meal and

conversations as they pleasantly observed our standing salutation to each other.

We heard their applause when we filed out after finishing our breakfast. I don't want to sound boastful, but we might well have anticipated it. We had, in that short week, grown accustomed to such accolades everywhere we went. We had become celebrities, heroes, even without uniforms of the Armed Forces or the hospital greens of a life-saving surgical team, or the garb of a NASA crew ready for a launch. Nor did we need helmets and shoulder pads to spin our way through the scrimmage lines of society. We moved around freely even with the usual entourage of well-wishers close at our heels.

Admittedly, we did get a few hard looks. Some misinformed people evidently thought we belonged to Hugh Hefner's playhouse partisans who were clad in street clothes, something entirely different than the usual mufti of their bedroom whirligigs.

With a lot of hard work, high resolve, and borrowed money, we had *Dos Piccolos* ready for the grand opening in late September.

The transaction was not velvety smooth, but it was effective.

We made sure Waco was ready for its newest and grandest Mexican restaurant. Going in, we knew our competition in the business would be fierce. So we advertised heavily and utilized a lot of promotional gimmicks. Brig did picturesque photography, and I supplied catchy material for ads in *The Clarion* and the local TV stations. We especially touted the

THE HELPERS

culinary skills of Carmela and Carmen. With great diligence, we also hired our staff for *Dos Piccolos*. I personally was delighted to hire Marie away from *Denney's* as our manager. She understood what we expected for our restaurant, and I knew she would convey those expectations to the staff people.

"You'll be for us what Eve Arden was for Joan Crawford in *Mildred Pierce*," I told her.

Marie smiled appreciatively. "I've always thought I resembled Eve Arden. Do you remember that spicy line of dialogue she said to Jack Carson in the movie?"

"No, I don't."

"That's good. I wouldn't want you to repeat it to your young bride."

Somehow amid the mad rush, Brig and I found the time to take our wives to their first American football game. Baylor lost, but our attendance at the stadium touched off a tumultuous standing ovation. The Golden Wave band played while the nimble cheerleaders performed some of their fancy spins and flings in honor of our presence.

"God, I just hope we're worthy of all this hoopla," I moaned to Brig.

"Better get used to it, Kandy. You have to realize we are now entrepreneurs, thanks to Carmen and Carmela. They have spun us into the Barnum and Bailey center ring, and there we bask in the spotlight. So let's soak up all the cheers we can before we become old age daredevils and take our high wire plunge into the Hospice net."

In October our thriving publicity carried us to a new highly acclaimed status.

On a bright, clear Saturday morning we were the honorary grand marshals in the Baylor homecoming parade through downtown Waco and the university campus. We rode in a gold convertible in which Carmela and Carmen were perched atop the back seat. During the long and spectacular parade, they kept playing the Baylor *alma mater* on their piccolos. Brig and I were seated beneath them, waving to the old grads and handing fresh hot tamales to spectators along the parade route. The parade ended in front of the Student Union Building.

When we climbed out of the convertible, our wives shivered. They wore low cut evening dresses that offered little warmth from the chill morning air. All through the parade, goose bumps dotted their skin, but that did not silence the piccolos. Carmela and Carmen happily endured the rigors of the crisp autumn morning. Brig and I were proud of them because they saw themselves as ambassadors of good will in appreciation for the way that Baylor and Waco continued the generous support of their new restaurant.

We hurried back to *Dos Piccolos* after the parade. A big noon crowd of Baylor exes greeted us, including the Reverend Dr. Geraud Collins and part of his family. He showered us with his usual gusto, but he also had a challenge for the twins.

"Ladies, this afternoon at the game, blow those piccolos long and loud. I predict that kind of performance will give the Bears a rousing boost and help them beat those pesky Aggies."

"We plan to hang them up in here at the entrance," said Carmen.

THE HELPERS

"Tomorrow will be soon enough for that," said Geraud. "Today they have a higher calling."

Brig and I agreed. We wanted that homecoming victory to cap off the dizzy pace we had set for ourselves following the double wedding in June. Any trick or gimmick that might seal that Baylor victory would be well worth the effort.

Carmen and Carmela realized that. In addition to their tantalizing Mexican food entrees, they gave the predominately alumni crowd a blaring sendoff to the game. They moved around from every table and booth piping their piccolos with the Baylor victory march, better known as *When The Saints Go Marching In*.

Brig and I stood proudly at the exit, greeting customers as they left.

"Sic 'em, Bears," we cried.

We grinned as Geraud approached. He shook our hands with the tent revival enthusiasm of a latter day *Elmer Gantry*. But Geraud Collins was no fictional character. He believed, absolutely and completely, that the piccolo twins would somehow help propel Baylor to victory that afternoon.

"Of course I believe that," he said without an ounce of modesty. "I have a pipeline to heaven, you should know by now, and I have it on the holy authority of Saint Peter himself that God loves piccolo music."

Brig and I became convinced that Geraud Collins indeed had Divine connections that memorable afternoon at the stadium. There the Bears confounded their bitter rivals from Texas A&M for the prized homecoming triumph.

We watched Carmen and Carmela take their place on the field with the Golden Wave Band as it cheered the large and happy Baylor throng with a blaring rendition of the victory march.

As we clapped our hands in response, Brig leaned over and spoke into my ear.

"I didn't realize our ladies knew how to play *Saints* on their piccolos."

"Neither did I. But we have to remember they have the uncanny smarts to accomplish anything they crave. They proved that when they made their trek to freedom from *Nuevo Laredo.*"

Brig nodded as the blaring serenade continued.

"And then we saw further proof of their intrepid style when they married us, didn't we? But they will never mother any children for us, will they?"

"Of course not," I shrugged. "Certain limitations do apply to anything and everything."

The band played on. Our Hedy Lamarr look-alikes were oblivious to our thoughts about them. Their piccolos continued to tweet their contribution to the rowdy victory celebration. The *Saints* were quite reluctant to march out into the post-game traffic clog surrounding the stadium.

Some of that traffic, we realized, would head for *Dos Piccolos*. Our memorable fun day was over. It would relinquish its magic to the Saturday evening hunger of the dinner patrons at the restaurant.

Brig and I began shuffling toward the nearest ramp. It was time for us to quickly find a vacant urinal in the men's restroom. That urinal, we hoped, would safely culminate our own victory march.

Chapter Twenty Seven
Rejoice and Be Glad

SPRINGTIME CAME TO WACO in 2001 with a verdant freshness and soft April breezes that chased away any lingering doubts about the arrival of the season.

On one of those afternoons when *Dos Piccolos* closed after the usual, heavy noon rush, Carmela insisted that we visit Lover's Leap again. I didn't know why, but I sensed that she needed to get away from the restaurant for awhile. Its popularity still meant a lot of work for us, even though we had hired additional staff people to help handle the daily bustle, including a morning clientele that kept flocking in with a fondness for our new breakfast menu that included *huevos rancheros*.

At Lover's Leap Carmela and I stood at the guard rail hand in hand as we viewed the surrounding vistas that were adorned in a variety of spring gowns. Down on the languid Bosque River, we spied a fish that twice leaped out of the water.

"Crazy fish," I remarked. "I'll never know why fish do those acrobatics."

"Maybe that fish is happy," Carmela smiled. "Perhaps he's just learned that he's going to be a father."

I spun around awkwardly on my heels to gaze at her face that brimmed with delight. Vividly, I recalled what she had said that day on our honeymoon.

"When we stood here last June as newlyweds, you said you wanted to return to this scenic spot when we had something worthy to share. Remember?"

She nibbled on me with a kiss, making sure that our faces measured each other with a winsome contact. In that closeness, Carmela spoke again.

"That's right, Homan dearest. It's only here in this beautiful place, that I would share my beautiful news with you. Here on this high ground, I want to lift you up to even higher ground. Sweetheart, you won't have to somersault out of the water like that fish did, but you're going to be a father."

"You're absolutely sure?"

"Of course. I'd still be over at *Dos Piccolos* in the kitchen if I wasn't sure."

I was wildly elated, but I tried to sound like the composite of dumb males who fashion themselves as knights protective of their wives when they have just learned about their impending fatherhood.

"You'll have to stay out of that kitchen from now on," I told her.

"Don't count on that, my love. Nor will I count on you acting your age while I make ready to present you with a son. I want you to feel young at heart. I want my pregnancy to be your fountain of youth. That old Ponce de Leon never found his, but you shall have yours. And I'm going to write about our parenthood. The chapters of that parenthood will be a gift, a cherished gift, our child someday will read and feel nobly blest."

THE HELPERS

"I feel nobly blest already," I told her. I hoped my lingering kiss informed her of the dimensions to which my blessing even then had extended.

We walked slowly back to our car, feeling immensely refreshed by the gorgeous April afternoon. We were also refreshed inwardly, knowing that having created a new life, we would receive new life.

"Does Carmen know?" I asked.

"Yes, and she's extremely happy about becoming an aunt. She hasn't told Brigdon, though. She'll leave that to you."

"I hate to pull rank on her and Brig with our news."

"They're family. You don't pull rank on family persons. You just share your good news with them. In turn, because they are family, they accept your joy with a gift of joy to you. That's a special bonus of love."

I looked at her with a rapturous smile. "Carmela, you will be a great mother and a great writer."

As we drove away from jagged Lover's Leap, I wondered how I would break the news to Brig about him becoming an uncle, or perhaps in the best sense, a godfather. When we neared the mouth of the Bosque, I decided what I would say. I would suggest to him that he load up his camera and be ready to get a snapshot of a proud fish plunging out of the river's flow.

He would, I was sure, think the suggestion was pure nonsense. But I was also sure Brig would then grasp my subtle humor like he always had.

When Carmela and I returned to *Dos Piccolos*, I stood with her for a silent moment gazing at the instruments locked crisscross with each other on the wall above the cashier's counter.

There they would always remain in honor, a reminder of the two young women Brigdon Chonliff and Homan Kandall had initially loved, Maydell Collins and Freddie Foster who had played them with such devotion and gifted ability.

But now Brig and I were hearing music that was different from the chirp of those piccolos. What we now heard was a melody that only Carmela and Carmen could bring to our aged lives with their brand of simplistic, nourishing love. The criss-crossed piccolos were a symbol of that love.

Like Julie Andrews as *Maria,* I knew Brig and I would once again be blest by the sound of music. Those Cameron Park hills were already alive with their anthems. But those choral hills would ultimately bow in surrender to the music of a new life in our midst with enchanting strains they could never duplicate.

In the dining area Brig and Carmen were dancing, much to the amusement of Geraud Collins who sat at one of the tables. The rhythmic clap of his hands spurred them on. It looked like a carnival scene on some parking lot after a big football game.

As if divinely directed, Geraud's presence in *Dos Piccolos* at that moment gave me a high plateau of inspiration. He always seemed to be around during my life's most enthralling moments. Now the champion of the Word was about to hear for himself another glorious version of the *Good News.* I would give it sound with all the laity splendor I could muster. I might not be one of his classroom *Beloveds,* but Geraud would surely show approval of my own brand of homiletic zeal. I could easily imagine him saying, when I finished , *Well done, good buddy. Now rejoice and be glad.*

I wanted Carmela to hear my sermon. I knew she would

furnish some very apt illustrations to it that would indeed cause us to rejoice and be glad.

But I never got to unload my homily with its introduction about the leaping fish in the Bosque River.

It was Geraud who leaped. He sprang to my side the moment Brig and Carmen stopped dancing. His hug was a touch of royalty.

"Good buddy, this dancing duo knows, and I know what you and Carmela have to tell us. We are thrilled to learn of her pre-natal condition. Congratulations."

"Kandy, I found out from Carmen," said Brig. "The way she kept clicking her castanets and twirling around in here this afternoon, I knew she had something important to say."

"I'm sorry, *hermana mia*," said Carmen. I just couldn't keep quiet any longer, especially when Dr. Collins arrived. I knew why you took Homan to Lover's Leap. We just had to go ahead and start celebrating."

"I even did a little two-step myself," said Geraud. "That's what King David did when he rescued the Ark and brought it safely back to Jerusalem. He had to celebrate and so did I."

"Well, Carmela and I want to join the celebration. Let's light up *Dos Piccolos* with a party tonight."

"We have something else to tell you two," smiled Carmen. "It will double the merrymaking. Tell them about the phone call, Brigdon."

"What phone call?" I asked.

"Oh, it wasn't much, just an announcement from the White House. The President is coming to Texas for a visit, and he and the First Lady want to include *Dos Piccolos* on their agenda while they're down here."

"Will they crave our Mexican food?" Carmela asked.

"Of course they will," I smiled to her. "They're both Texans."

I turned to Geraud. "Good buddy, did you have anything to do with that phone call?"

"Not really. Oh, in a faculty meeting I may have thought out loud that such a visit would be a crown jewel for *Dos Piccolos*, but it was some Baylor people with heavy clout who picked up the ball and ran with it."

All of us knew we had to forget Carmela's pregnancy and the presidential visit for awhile. The afternoon was swiftly drifting away. That meant we had to be sure *Dos Piccolos* was ready for the early evening rush when our staff people reported for work.

I took Carmela by the hand as we walked with Geraud to the entrance. When he left, I stood with her looking again at the criss-crossed piccolos.

"Will they ever make music again?" I asked.

"They are making music right now, my dearest. Listen and you will hear them in the full orchestra that has captured the sweep of our melodic love."

Her flow of words told me once more that her writing career would one day charm the souls of countless people.

One of those persons, I envisioned, would be our son, tall and stalwart with an elflock of dark hair. His name would be Paul Brigdon Kandall, and he like his mother and his loving aunt, would in some remarkable manner become a worthy helper to a needy impaired segment of the human race.

THE END

CPSIA information can be obtained at www.ICGtesting.com
Printed in the USA
LVOW06s2242171114

414216LV00001B/113/P